A WINNER NEVER QUITS *and* A QUITTER NEVER WINS!

A WINNER NEVER QUITS

and

A QUITTER NEVER WINS!

LEE ROBERSON

SWORD of the LORD
PUBLISHERS
P.O. BOX 1099, MURFREESBORO, TN 37133

Printed and Bound in the United States of America

Dedication

Dedicated to the memory of a man who never quit—Paul the apostle.

Also, to the memory of Mrs. Daisy Hawes, the Sunday schoolteacher who pointed me to Christ;

and to the hundreds of preachers where I have ministered in the United States and foreign countries.

Contents

Foreword

In this book I am reviewing my sixty-six years in the ministry. I am recalling experiences of all kinds—good, bad and indifferent. Without apology, I am repeating outlines I have given in hundreds of churches, both in America and in many foreign lands.

I will be thinking back over my forty years and six months as pastor of the Highland Park Baptist Church, as well as my years in other churches, plus more than eleven years preaching in more than 1300 churches since I retired.

INTRODUCTION

The title of this book is not original—"A winner never quits, and a quitter never wins." I have heard it most of my life. I have used it on myself when the going got tough. Now, at almost 85, I still use it. I may change my address soon, but I am not quitting. Praise God, through faith in Christ, I have everlasting life!

But many quit! Preachers quit, missionaries quit, Sunday schoolteachers quit, deacons quit, ushers quit. All of us need to hear the words of the Apostle Paul: "Therefore, my beloved brethren, be ye stedfast, unmoveable, always abounding in the work of the Lord..." (I Cor. 15:58).

Our Lord didn't quit! He went to the cross for us. He is interceding for us now.

Keep on going!

Dr. Lee Roberson

WHERE I BEGAN IN 1930

My first pastorate—Germantown Baptist Church, Germantown, Tennessee

PHILLIPS MEMORIAL CHAPEL
In 1942, when I came, this was the church.

THE TABERNACLE

Completed in 1947; named Chauncey-Goode Auditorium in 1981

HIGHLAND PARK BAPTIST CHURCH
Auditorium completed in 1981

Full house in new auditorium, September, 1981

Part I
Sermons

The Winner

"I have fought a good fight, I have finished my course, I have kept the faith."—II Tim. 4:7.

The world loves a winner. A good loser may be popular for a time, but eventually his place will be taken by a winner. We like winning football teams and baseball teams, and even the most peaceful of people will give some deference to a winning prize fighter. We like to see a man win in the battle of life. He may not attain to riches or popular glory, but there is something about him that proclaims he is a winner.

Babe Ruth was a champion. They say he knocked more than seven hundred home runs in his dramatic and colorful career on the baseball diamond. We sometimes forget that he struck out a thousand times. His closing days were somewhat painful; and he came to the end of his life in weakness. But he was known as a winner, a champion.

The Apostle Paul was a winner. There were about him all the attributes of the victorious man.

Now, let us consider this under three headings.

I. PAUL KNEW THAT HE WAS A WINNER

"I have fought a good fight, I have finished my course, I have kept the faith." A man can know when he has won in the battle of life. This is not egotism. This is a sense of understanding what God wanted him to do and a knowledge that the task has been done. Paul had an inner feeling of peace that always comes to the one who does his best.

Paul gave his statement of victory from the prison cell. The words of our text were doubtless written down a short time before his death. This means that circumstances at the close of life don't determine a man's victory or lack of it.

A man might have much of this world's goods and still be a failure. He might be acclaimed by men as a success, as a winner, but still be a failure.

I remember reading some time ago about ten of the world's most successful financiers who died as miserable failures. They may have had money when they came to the end of life; but some of them, in the desperation of existing circumstances, committed suicide.

When Paul sat in the Roman jail, he knew that his life had been well spent. He knew that he was a winner.

1. *He was a winner because of obedience.* From the Damascus road experience, his life was under the domination of Jesus Christ.

Paul obeyed Christ when it meant much suffering. He worked at his tent-making during the day and preached from a fervent heart at night. He was a man of prayer. He sought relief from the thorn in the flesh; but when God decided that it should remain, he took the decision gladly. As a result, he came to a glorious, victorious end.

2. *Paul was a winner in his faithfulness.* Paul could look back over his life and remember the victories gained through his faithful witnessing. His calling was a simple one: to be a witness for Jesus. Everywhere he went he gave a testimony of the Saviour. When he stood before the Sanhedrin or when he talked before Felix or Agrippa, he poured out his heart and witnessed faithfully.

3. *He was a winner in dissatisfaction.* Don't be confused by this statement. I simply mean to say that Paul was never satisfied. He was always pressing on to do more for Christ: ". . . this one thing I do, forgetting those things which are behind, and reaching forth unto

those things which are before, I press toward the mark for the prize of the high calling of God in Christ Jesus."

The man is a loser who relaxes and says, "I've got it made." We must keep on working, keep on striving, keep moving forward.

4. *Paul was a winner in peace.* Since the peace of God filled his heart, he was able to tell others how to have peace. Paul could say, "Be careful for nothing; but in every thing by prayer and supplication with thanksgiving let your requests be made known unto God. And the peace of God, which passeth all understanding, shall keep your hearts and minds through Christ Jesus."

Knowing he was a winner, he could say with confidence and without boasting, "I have fought a good fight, I have finished my course, I have kept the faith."

II. CHRISTIANS OF ALL AGES AGREE THAT PAUL WAS A WINNER

The first century bowed before him, knowing he was a man of God. Kings listened to him. Common people heard him gladly. Leaders of men were attracted to him and acknowledged his position.

Christians of all centuries have been blessed and inspired when hearing the name Paul.

1. *He was a winner by his life.* His life was clean, circumspect and upright. He lived for Christ, as Christ lived in him.

Worldliness had no part in his life. He might have been attracted a few times by the enticing works of men's hands, but we find no evidence that he turned aside. He saw much of the known world. He had a versatile brain, a fervent tongue, a compassionate heart— and used all in the service of Christ. Some dropped by the wayside in Paul's day, but he walked on.

2. *Paul was a winner by his writings.* Placing himself in the hands of Christ, he could leave something for this world. The Pauline epistles, inspired by the Holy Spirit, have a great place in the world's greatest Book. Today Paul is read and quoted throughout every portion of the world. His inspired writings are used as guides for both churches and individuals. In his letters we find practical advice for

the individual (read I Thess. 5:15–23). We find, also, comfort in his writings (read I Cor. 15; I Thess. 4). In his writings are words to guide the local church.

Two thousand years have not dimmed nor subtracted from the worthiness of the words written by Paul.

3. *He was a winner by his personal work.* The greatest task given to anyone is that of spreading the Gospel. It is for us to tell the good news of salvation. No life is wasted that is given to this task. At all times, under all circumstances, Paul witnessed. Sometimes in our timidity and fear, we turn aside from the golden opportunities presented to us. Not so with Paul. Faithfully he gave forth the message of Christ.

III. THE LOST WORLD AGREES THAT PAUL WAS A WINNER

In the day of the apostle, sinners agreed that his life was victorious. Men trembled under the impact of his testimony. Felix trembled. Festus was impressed. Agrippa said, "Almost thou persuadest me to be a Christian."

Paul was a winner of lost souls. Many heard his message and turned to Christ. Nothing better can be said about anyone than this: "He is a winner of souls."

When the Holy Spirit called Barnabas and Saul for the work of missions, they began at once to testify. On the Isle of Cyprus they won a convert. In every place many believed in Jesus Christ.

Of course, many did not receive the Lord; but they, too, had to agree that Paul was a winner. They knew that there was something different about this man. They knew he was fighting an adversary, even Satan.

The lost sometimes have more perception of certain matters than Christians. Men could see that Paul was fighting the enemy of all enemies. Paul had no more doubt of a personal Devil than he had of God. He knew that Satan was fighting against him at every turn and seeking to keep him from doing God's will.

Paul went on to be victorious in Asia Minor, in Greece, in Rome;

yea, everywhere people knew him to be a man of God.

In death, the lost world acknowledged his victory. I don't believe Paul had a tremor of fear as he came to the end. Our text indicates that there was complete trust and a resting upon the promises of God as he faced death.

"I have finished my course," said he. Many start but not many finish victoriously. We saw young people start in Tennessee Temple Schools and then turn aside, sometimes through lack of faith or because of discouraging words of others. A few days ago I met a young lady who had attended our school for awhile, then stopped. She told me that one of the big regrets of her life was not completing her work.

Finish the course. Don't be deterred by criticism nor be allured by the enticing evils of this world.

A pastor in the West had an applauding world at his feet. To maintain his reputation for friendliness and being a man's man, he emptied his wine glass at many banquets. Instead of refusing alcoholic drinks, he became an alcoholic. He was guarded by his faithful and hopeful members but finally died a victim of liquor. He didn't finish the course!

Yesterday's paper told of a man who was blown to pieces in the airport in Wichita, Kansas. They said he was despondent, sad, sick, and without work. What a sad way to finish the course of life!

I like better that which was done by a certain preacher. He had been successful in his work, yet he came to the end of life while still young. Concerning the last day of his life, his wife said:

> When he knew he couldn't live through the day, he called his three children to his bedside and chatted with them as though they were going off to school and he would see them the same as usual when they got back.
>
> But when they left the room, he said to me, "I don't want them to see me again. When they saw me last, my hands were warm on theirs. I could smile. My eyes were alive with life. I don't want them to see me dead. When they see me again, because of the mercy of God and the resurrection power of my Saviour, I will be alive."

That is a better way to close out life than the way of the poor man who blew himself into eternity in the airport.

One day we are going to see Paul, this man who was a winner, this man whose name has been known for the last nineteen centuries, the one who said, "I have finished my course, I have kept the faith," the one who didn't vary. To the end, Paul was a picture of faithfulness, stability and vigor.

Are you ready to meet God? Do you know Christ as your Saviour? Are you trusting in Him? Is eternal life sure for you?

A funeral was being held on a wind-swept hillside, twenty-five miles from the railroad. A little girl came up to the funeral director who had had the mother's funeral some three months before and said, "Mister, I want to know what you did with my mother."

What a beautiful thing he could say to her: "Your mother is now in Heaven."

2

Demas
the Quitter

"For Demas hath forsaken me, having loved this present world, and is departed unto Thessalonica; Crescens to Galatia, Titus unto Dalmatia.

"Only Luke is with me. Take Mark, and bring him with thee: for he is profitable to me for the ministry.

"And Tychicus have I sent to Ephesus."—II Tim. 4:10–12.

This male sextet of the first century was composed of Demas, Crescens, Titus, Luke, Mark and Tychicus.

Demas is mentioned three times in the Bible. In Colossians 4:14 we read: "Luke, the beloved physician, and Demas, greet you." In Philemon 24 we read, "Marcus, Aristarchus, Demas, Lucas, my fellowlabourers." And here in II Timothy 4:10 Demas is mentioned.

Crescens is mentioned only here in II Timothy 4:10.

Titus is mentioned eleven times in II Corinthians, Galatians and II Timothy.

Luke, the faithful physician, is mentioned only a few times by name: in Colossians 4:14, Philemon 24, and here in II Timothy. But the name of Luke, the beloved physician, is known wherever the Gospel is given. The Gospel of Luke makes his name immortal.

Mark is mentioned a number of times—the young man who failed

Paul in the first missionary journey, the one who came back to God and became a success in spiritual work. The Gospel of Mark came from his inspired pen.

Tychicus is mentioned five times in the Bible: in Acts 20:4, Ephesians 6:21, Colossians 4:7, II Timothy 4:12, and Titus 3:12. This man excelled in faithfulness and achieved a place of eternal significance by his alignment with Paul.

All these men were close to the Apostle Paul.

1. *Paul was the man of dissatisfaction.* He always desired to do more, to accomplish more. He was concerned with preaching and pressing on. By this dissatisfaction, Paul is a blessing to all men.

The one who has arrived and is thoroughly satisfied in life is never a blessing to the world. We do need a steady tread of the wise conservative to offset the foolish lunging of the radical. But most of all, we need men who are dissatisfied with themselves and their accomplishments; and because of this, they press on.

2. *Paul was the man of direction.* He forgot about the past and looked to the future. The nation that lives in the past is finished. The company is done that looks backward. The Christian is powerless who can talk only of the "good old days." We are to be men of direction—forward direction.

3. *Paul was the man of dedication.* We can best say it in these words: he was sold out to God and to God's work. Because of his dedication, he could cry out to the world, "I beseech you therefore, brethren, by the mercies of God, that ye present your bodies a living sacrifice, holy, acceptable unto God, which is your reasonable service" (Rom. 12:1).

Now look again at this sextet. Every man has his place. God places an importance on the individual. Crescens, Titus, Luke, Mark, Tychicus had their places of work. They were moving forward in their tasks.

But wait! The sextet had broken harmony, broken by one voice, the voice of Demas. The sextet should have been complete; instead, it lacked one. Paul tells us about this man: "Demas hath forsaken me, having loved this present world, and is departed unto Thessalonica."

Demas must have said to Paul, "I quit. I'm going home."

In Colossians 4:14 Paul spoke of Demas in a kindly way, mentioning his name alongside that of Luke, the beloved physician. In Philemon 24 he called Demas "his fellowlabourer."

What happened to Demas? We can give you the answer from the Word of God.

I. HE LOVED THIS PRESENT WORLD

We cannot argue this, because it is plainly stated by Paul himself. Demas apparently got too close to this world. Many times he had heard Paul preach about putting on the whole armor of God and shunning the very appearance of evil.

But somehow he forgot to do what he heard. His mind became fixed with matters in Thessalonica. Perhaps he began to think about his former work. He may have left his home in the care of others, and he thought of going back to his favorite easy chair and good food. Again, maybe his thought was on his former companions and how good it would be to join in their company and enjoy life with them. Or he may have thought of his business and dreamed of the days when he could be back home, smiling and shaking hands with those who would come in to do business with him.

When one gets saved, the only way of safety is to cut loose from the world and all entangling alliances. Make a clean break with the past. Face it and march forward with Him.

I was reading about the man who had committed what he thought was the perfect murder. He carried the dead man out of his house through the back way, placed him on the front seat of the car, and let him lean against the car door as if he were asleep.

It was night when he drove through the city to the seaside. He placed some weights around the dead man's body and carried it on his back out into the sea. Going as far as he dared, he tried to free the dead man from his back to dump him into the sea; but because rigor mortis had set in, the arms of the corpse wouldn't let go of the man's neck. And he couldn't free himself from the legs of the corpse, for they were wrapped around his waist.

The dead man went out into the sea all right, but he took a live one with him.

Things of earth get hold of a man and damage his Christian life. We are admonished not to love this present world. Listen to these words:

"Love not the world, neither the things that are in the world. If any man love the world, the love of the Father is not in him.

"For all that is in the world, the lust of the flesh, and the lust of the eyes, and the pride of life, is not of the Father, but is of the world.

"And the world passeth away, and the lust thereof: but he that doeth the will of God abideth for ever."—I John 2:15–17.

II. DEMAS LACKED STRONG CHRISTIAN CONVICTIONS

This is plainly what Paul is saying. He doesn't say that Demas was a lost man. The evidence points to the fact that Demas had been saved but had turned away from working with Paul and had gone home. His convictions were weak!

Oh, the importance of Christian convictions! No man ever accomplishes much without strong convictions. Especially is this true in the field of Christian service.

This day calls for convictions—convictions on right and wrong. This season of the year will be the testing time for many. The Devil will be walking about seeking whom he may devour, testing every child of God. He will place before everyone the testing elements of this evil world. This is the time for convictions.

This day calls for convictions regarding the truth. Have convictions about the Lord Jesus Christ. Believe that He is the one and only Saviour. Proclaim Him as Saviour, Lord and Master.

One of the companies in Chattanooga has placed signboards in various places which read: CHRISTMAS IS CHRIST'S BIRTHDAY. That to me is very understandable, but some people don't realize this.

For example, I had sent to me the *Weekly Reader*, a children's newspaper. Page 1 gives a line: "Christmas News: Christmas Is a Happy Time." In the *Weekly Reader*, one page is devoted to a letter to children from the editor-in-chief. She entitles the letter: "Christmas in the Public Schools." It reads:

Dear Colleague:

Christmas is essentially a religious feast. It commemorates an event of great religious significance. For this reason, teachers must take special care not to violate the constitutional right of religious freedom of any pupil by the way Christmas is celebrated in school.

On the other hand, Christmas is a joyous and festive season that is traditionally a part of our heritage. At this time of the year Christmas music is heard from all quarters. Public places are aglow with lights from Christmas trees and decorations. There is a pervasive feeling of goodwill in the air. A child remembers this atmosphere when he leaves it to enter the school.

While the birth of Christ has great historical importance in Western civilization, public schools obviously cannot observe Christmas as a religious feast. Teaching the religious significance of Christmas should be reserved for the home or place of worship.

However, schools cannot ignore Christmas as if the season did not exist. Many schools may schedule programs that might include:

—Knowledge of differing Christmas family observances and loyalties.
—Discovery of the different community and folk customs and traditions of Christmas.
—Appreciation of these differing beliefs and customs.
—Knowledge and appreciation of cross-cultural customs and ideas about Christmas in other lands.
—Exposure to the wealth of artistic, literary, musical and dramatic works that are directly related to Christmas.

At Christmastime, more than at any other time of year, men's thoughts turn to the universal idea of peace on earth, goodwill to men. Use this time of year to develop the idea of universal peace and goodwill to bring us all a little closer to this ideal.

Cordially yours,

Editor-in-Chief
My Weekly Reader

This is America, a land founded by Christians. This is the country where men came so they might read the Word of God and worship God the Father, the Lord Jesus Christ and the Holy Spirit.

Now we are advised to turn away from all such ideas. We can talk about Christmas, but we must not speak about Christ. We are to think now about "universal peace on earth." We must try to "develop the idea of universal peace and goodwill."

What tragic foolishness and ignorance! There can be no peace without the Lord Jesus Christ, the Prince of Peace. There can be no goodwill unless men turn to the Saviour. The message is the same for Jew and Gentile, for Catholic and Protestant. There is one message—the message of Jesus Christ, the Son of God.

This day calls for convictions about right and wrong and especially convictions about the Saviour. This Bible declares, "Neither is there salvation in any other: for there is none other name under heaven given among men, whereby we must be saved" (Acts 4:12).

Demas lacked strong convictions; consequently, he turned back. The twentieth century is sorely like Demas—lacking in convictions.

III. HE NEEDED PLAIN, SIMPLE FAITH IN GOD

No one can reach the heights of spiritual greatness without faith in God. I speak of a real, telling faith based on the living and written Word.

No man can obtain things from God without faith. Believing prayer is based on faith. "If ye have faith as a grain of mustard seed, ye shall say unto this mountain, Remove hence to yonder place; and it shall remove; and nothing shall be impossible unto you" (Matt. 17:20).

There is nothing very spectacular about a grain of mustard seed. Ah, but the Lord is teaching something. The mustard seed, though small, may be planted into the ground, and billions of little atoms are at work rearranging themselves in creating the first cells of the mustard tree. The days pass and a tiny plant breaks through the soil. Higher and higher the little plant shoots up.

Mustard seed faith is not a spectacular faith, but it is an unrelenting faith, the faith that Jesus said will move the mountains.

No man can endure opposition without faith. The world will come against us. We will be opposed, persecuted, ridiculed. But when we have faith, we can stand up and go straight forward.

It may be that, because poor Demas couldn't stand the opposition and persecution of the world, he turned back.

No man can bear bodily suffering without faith. In recent days I have had pressed upon me the testimony of a number of Christians who are going through special suffering. I have been noticing the quiet serenity of their minds and the positive notes of their words.

Suffering? Yes. But bear it through faith in God.

No man can bear the sorrows of life without faith. How suddenly the peacefulness of your home can be disturbed! How quickly the tranquility of your mind can break under some sorrow!

Yesterday I made a visit to the Children's Hospital. A number of black people were standing in silence at the doorway of the first floor.

I made my calls and came out. As I left the door, I noticed that some of the black people were crying. As they moved out across the parking lot, I went up to them and said, "Is there something I can do? Has someone been seriously injured?" A man said, "Her child was killed," pointing to the mother.

I tried to give a few comforting words; then I said, "Let us pause right here and pray." As I began to pray, the sobs ceased. The men removed their hats and bowed their heads. In the darkness I prayed that God would comfort them in this time of sorrow.

I repeat: no man can bear life's sorrows without faith. I know the awful emptiness of the soul when the death message is given. We must have Christ and have faith in Him.

But Demas turned away. By his turning, he lost the companionship of Paul and the fellowship of Christ and many Christians. How foolish the one who turns from the Saviour! With all of his needs, how ridiculous that poor little man who would turn his back upon the Christ who can supply every need. Yet Demas turned away. He left Paul and went back to his former home. Why? ". . . having loved this present world. . . ."

It has been said, "Christ may exhaust the universe, but the universe will never exhaust Christ." Julian, the apostate, learned this on the field of battle. Julian was a Roman emperor for four years.

He attempted to restore paganism to the Roman Empire at the expense of Christianity.

This well-educated man wrote a book entitled *The Banquet of the Caesars.* He advanced deep into Persian territory about A.D. 362.

One day he turned to a Christian soldier and asked, "What do you suppose your friend Jesus is doing today?"

The soldier answered, "Sir, since Jesus is a carpenter, it may be that even today He is taking time off from building mansions for the faithful to build a coffin for you."

On that day Julian's army was outnumbered and surrounded by the Persians. In the bloody battle, he was seriously wounded and died within a few hours. Shortly before his death, he gathered up the dust of the battlefield that was clotted with his own blood and, flinging it toward the heavens, cried, "O Galilean, Thou hast conquered!"

Demas turned away from the One who could conquer sin, death and the grave. I say to you, my friend, it is time that you turn to the Saviour, time that you believe in Jesus Christ. There is no time to waste. Come to Jesus now. Receive Him today.

A boy told this story about his grandparents and his uncle.

The telephone rang. Grandmother, nearest to the phone, picked it up. "Hello." She listened for the reply. "Long distance?" she repeated in a quavering voice. Then aside to Grandpa, who had moved closer, "It is a long distance call, Father. It must be from Jim. Here, you take it. I'm afraid I can't hear a word he is saying."

Jim called his parents to say he was too busy with his own affairs to come home for Christmas. Things had come up at the last minute.

He couldn't see the tears in Grandmother's eyes; and maybe he didn't hear the tremor in Grandpa's voice as the old man said quietly, "Yes, Jim, I understand. You come as soon as you can."

When the old people sat down again by the fire, the boy went over to his grandmother and said, "Isn't Uncle Jim coming?" She shook her head. "Says he is too busy."

Jim didn't come home that Christmas or the next. He didn't come because he didn't want to.

The boy, about twelve years old, said the phone rang the day before Christmas. He answered it. The operator said, "Long distance calling." Since he was alone in the home, the boy took the call and felt very important doing so.

He heard a somewhat familiar voice, a voice out of the past. "Is that you, Johnny?" He answered, "Yes. Who is this?" He already knew it was Uncle Jim. And when his uncle said the words that he had said years ago, the boy answered, "It's no use coming, Uncle Jim. You're too late. They have gone."

I give that simple illustration to remind you that time is passing away. When death comes, it is too late. When suddenly life is snuffed out, it is too late. Now is the time to repent and believe and come to the Saviour.

"Behold, now is the accepted time; behold, now is the day of salvation."—II Cor. 6:2.

3

If I
Should Die
Before He Comes

"And as it is appointed unto men once to die, but after this the judgment. . . ."—Heb. 9:27.

"And if I go and prepare a place for you, I will come again, and receive you unto myself; that where I am, there ye may be also."—John 14:3.

For many months I have had a long white envelope on my desk at home. On the front of the envelope are the words, *"If I should die before He comes."*

Inside I have given brief directions for my funeral—"if I should die before He comes."

I have chosen the funeral home. (I hope they don't go out of business.)

I have chosen the participants for the service.

I have chosen the length of the service.

I have chosen the songs and singers.

I have chosen the place of burial (not too many yards from where our daughter Joy is buried).

I have made all of these simple suggestions to help my dear

family—my wife, children and grandchildren—in the event that I die before He comes! I am looking for His return. I would rather go up into His presence than down into the grave.

"But I would not have you to be ignorant, brethren, concerning them which are asleep, that ye sorrow not, even as others which have no hope.

"For if we believe that Jesus died and rose again, even so them also which sleep in Jesus will God bring with him.

"For this we say unto you by the word of the Lord, that we which are alive and remain unto the coming of the Lord shall not prevent them which are asleep.

"For the Lord himself shall descend from heaven with a shout, with the voice of the archangel, and with the trump of God: and the dead in Christ shall rise first:

"Then we which are alive and remain shall be caught up together with them in the clouds, to meet the Lord in the air: and so shall we ever be with the Lord.

"Wherefore comfort one another with these words."—I Thess. 4:13–18.

Permit me to give you four simple thoughts:

I. WISE PEOPLE MAKE READY FOR TWO CERTAIN EVENTS— DEATH OR THE SECOND COMING

"And as it is appointed unto men once to die, but after this the judgment." Christ said, "Watch therefore, for ye know neither the day nor the hour wherein the Son of man cometh" (Matt. 25:13).

Both facts are laid before us in the Scriptures: death and the Second Coming. No one can deny the simple and understandable words of Christ. There is no mystery about death or the Second Coming.

But we must be ready for these sure events. Thousands die daily throughout the world. We are exhorted to "prepare to meet thy God."

Keep in mind that we are eternal souls, souls that will spend eternity in Heaven or in Hell.

"There was a certain rich man, which was clothed in purple and

fine linen, and fared sumptuously every day:

"And there was a certain beggar named Lazarus, which was laid at his gate, full of sores,

"And desiring to be fed with the crumbs which fell from the rich man's table: moreover the dogs came and licked his sores.

"And it came to pass, that the beggar died, and was carried by the angels into Abraham's bosom: the rich man also died, and was buried;

"And in hell he lift up his eyes, being in torments, and seeth Abraham afar off, and Lazarus in his bosom.

"And he cried and said, Father Abraham, have mercy on me, and send Lazarus, that he may dip the tip of his finger in water, and cool my tongue; for I am tormented in this flame.

"But Abraham said, Son, remember that thou in thy lifetime receivedst thy good things, and likewise Lazarus evil things: but now he is comforted, and thou art tormented.

"And beside all this, between us and you there is a great gulf fixed: so that they which would pass from hence to you cannot; neither can they pass to us, that would come from thence.

"Then he said, I pray thee therefore, father, that thou wouldest send him to my father's house:

"For I have five brethren; that he may testify unto them, lest they also come into this place of torment.

"Abraham saith unto him, They have Moses and the prophets; let them hear them.

"And he said, Nay, father Abraham: but if one went unto them from the dead, they will repent.

"And he said unto him, If they hear not Moses and the prophets, neither will they be persuaded, though one rose from the dead."— Luke 16:19–31.

Heaven is the eternal home of all who put their faith in Christ.

"Let not your heart be troubled: ye believe in God, believe also in me.

"In my Father's house are many mansions: if it were not so, I would have told you. I go to prepare a place for you.

"And if I go and prepare a place for you, I will come again, and

receive you unto myself; that where I am, there ye may be also.

"And whither I go ye know, and the way ye know.

"Thomas saith unto him, Lord, we know not whither thou goest; and how can we know the way?

"Jesus saith unto him, I am the way, the truth, and the life: no man cometh unto the Father, but by me."—John 14:1-6.

"For God so loved the world, that he gave his only begotten Son, that whosoever believeth in him should not perish, but have everlasting life."—John 3:16.

"He that believeth on him is not condemned: but he that believeth not is condemned already, because he hath not believed in the name of the only begotten Son of God."—John 3:18.

"He that believeth on the Son hath everlasting life: and he that believeth not the Son shall not see life; but the wrath of God abideth on him."—John 3:36.

An humble sweet Sunday schoolteacher made me aware of my need. When I attended her class of intermediate boys, Mrs. Daisy Hawes gave me the gospel message. After listening to her for two Sundays, I settled this important matter in my home the following week.

I knew I was a sinner, unredeemed, lost. When I heard the message of salvation from God's eternal Word, I received Christ as my Saviour. "But as many as received him, to them gave he power to become the sons of God, even to them that believe on his name" (John 1:12).

Now, on the basis of God's eternal, infallible Word, I have eternal life. God said it; I believe it! I am saved, not because I live better or behave better or serve better—no! I am saved by my faith in Jesus Christ who died in my place on the cross.

II. WISE PEOPLE SERVE GOD IN HUMBLE GRATITUDE FOR THE GREAT GIFT OF SALVATION

Salvation—the new birth—makes you a new creature. "Therefore if any man be in Christ, he is a new creature: old things are passed away; behold, all things are become new" (II Cor. 5:17).

Let us begin with the primary matter of worship. Every thinking Christian should desire to worship God. How can we best do that? By church attendance Sunday morning, Sunday evening, and Wednesday evening prayer service. "Not forsaking the assembling of ourselves together, as the manner of some is; but exhorting one another: and so much the more, as ye see the day approaching" (Heb. 10:25).

Going to church to worship God, going to church to express your gratitude for His blessings, going to church to learn more about God's Word and God's will, seems such an elementary matter. Yet many thousands of professing Christians rarely enter the doors of God's house. Perhaps many profess but are not saved. But many who are saved miss the amazing joy of worship and fellowship.

Again, worshiping God out of a grateful heart means the giving of our means to His work. We give because we love. We give because we want others to have the same joy we have.

Every Christian should be a tither. This means giving one-tenth of your income to the Lord's work at home and on mission fields.

Notice the words of Malachi 3:9-11:

"Ye are cursed with a curse: for ye have robbed me, even this whole nation.

"Bring ye all the tithes into the storehouse, that there may be meat in mine house, and prove me now herewith, saith the Lord of hosts, if I will not open you the windows of heaven, and pour you out a blessing, that there shall not be room enough to receive it.

"And I will rebuke the devourer for your sakes, and he shall not destroy the fruits of your ground; neither shall your vine cast her fruit before the time in the field, saith the Lord of hosts."

Multitudes testify to the blessings, both spiritually and materially, of tithing. Don't let selfishness cheat you out of this blessing.

III. WISE PEOPLE PRAY!

In general, most people believe in prayer, but sadly so few actually pray! "Lord, teach us to pray."

Too many who believe in prayer form certain habits of reciting prayers without the consciousness of talking to their eternal Heavenly Father.

The recitation of certain prayerful words achieves a result, but we are not reaching Heaven with our needs. I refer to the invocation at the beginning of a service, the offertory prayer as we receive the offering, and the benediction given as people gather up their coats and hats to leave the house of God. The invocation, the offertory prayer and the benediction, which are a formal part of most services, can be real and effective; but generally they are given repetitiously and without heart content.

Wise people pray! We pray because we need God's guidance, God's strength, and, most of all, God's presence.

What blessed examples are given to us of prayer!

Abraham prayed:

"Abram called on the name of the Lord."—Gen. 13:4.

Moses prayed repeatedly:

"And Moses said unto the Lord, See, thou sayest unto me, Bring up this people: and thou hast not let me know whom thou wilt send with me. Yet thou hast said, I know thee by name, and thou hast also found grace in my sight.

"Now therefore, I pray thee, if I have found grace in thy sight, shew me now thy way, that I may know thee, that I may find grace in thy sight: and consider that this nation is thy people.

"And he said, My presence shall go with thee, and I will give thee rest."—Exod. 33:12–14.

Elijah prayed:

"Hear me, O Lord, hear me, that this people may know that thou art the Lord God, and that thou hast turned their heart back again.

"Then the fire of the Lord fell, and consumed the burnt-sacrifice, and the wood, and the stones, and the dust, and licked up the water that was in the trench.

"And when all the people saw it, they fell on their faces: and they said, The Lord, he is the God; the Lord, he is the God."—I Kings 18:37–39.

Isaiah prayed:

"Also I heard the voice of the Lord, saying, Whom shall I send, and who will go for us? Then said I, Here am I; send me."—Isa. 6:8.

Jeremiah prayed:

"Ah Lord God! behold, thou hast made the heaven and the earth by thy great power and stretched out arm, and there is nothing too hard for thee."—Jer. 32:17.

Our Lord Jesus prayed:

"Father, if thou be willing, remove this cup from me: nevertheless not my will, but thine, be done."—Luke 22:42.

Yes, wise people pray, and God answers prayers!

Bring every need before Him.

He will guide you: "I will guide thee with mine eye" (Ps. 32:8).

He will supply your needs: "But my God shall supply all your need according to his riches in glory by Christ Jesus" (Phil. 4:19).

He will give us peace of heart: "Peace I leave with you, my peace I give unto you: not as the world giveth, give I unto you. Let not your heart be troubled, neither let it be afraid" (John 14:27).

I exhort you to pray about every need—better still, to pray about everything!

Pray daily that you will die to self. Paul confessed, "I die daily." In Romans 6:11 he admonishes, "Likewise reckon ye also yourselves to be dead indeed unto sin, but alive unto God through Jesus Christ our Lord."

Pray daily that you may be filled with the Holy Spirit. The early Christians who lived and died so victoriously were filled; and we, too, can be filled. "And be not drunk with wine, wherein is excess; but be filled with the Spirit" (Eph. 5:18).

Yes, wise people pray!

IV. WISE PEOPLE WITNESS

"But ye shall receive power, after that the Holy Ghost is come upon you: and ye shall be witnesses unto me both in Jerusalem, and in all

Judaea, and in Samaria, and unto the uttermost part of the earth."—
Acts 1:8.

The greatest event in your life was your salvation. When you were saved, you became a new creature, a child of God. You received the Holy Spirit, who abides in your heart. Your name was written down in the Lamb's book of life. You were eternally saved. "And I give unto them eternal life; and they shall never perish, neither shall any man pluck them out of my hand" (John 10:28).

Through faith in Christ, you are a child of God! Remember Ephesians 2:8, 9: "For by grace are ye saved through faith; and that not of yourselves: it is the gift of God: Not of works, lest any man should boast."

Now, the command of God is for you to tell of your salvation, to bear witness to His saving grace.

Your salvation is not to be hidden away! You are to tell it abroad by your speech and life.

I could never forget the Sunday morning at Highland Park Baptist Church when a rough, bearded man beyond middle age came to the altar to be saved. His clothing was old, soiled and tattered. I had part in leading him to Christ.

I went back to the platform and continued the invitation for others to come and be saved. I looked to one side; and there on the platform stood the dirty, bearded man I had just led to the Lord. Tears were trickling down his grimy face.

He walked over to me and gave me a gentle push, saying, "Preacher, let me tell them what it means to be saved. I can do it better than you can."

When one is saved, he wants others to be saved also. When the wife gets saved, she wants the husband to be saved, too. When parents get saved, they want their children to be saved.

Are you a child of God? Then tell it everywhere! Jesus said, "Let your light so shine before men, that they may see your good works, and glorify your Father which is in heaven" (Matt. 5:16).

Witness by your life! So live that others know you are saved! Don't be ashamed to stand up for Him!

Witness by your lips! Tell others about Him! Tell what you know. If you know that Christ saved you, then tell it. We are all different, but the way to get saved is the same for all. "For I delivered unto you first of all that which I also received, how that Christ died for our sins according to the scriptures" (I Cor. 15:3).

You may be young, you may be old; you may be educated, you may be uneducated; you may be cultured, you may be crude—but God will use your testimony of your faith in Christ.

I knew a man who never finished the third grade in school, but he was a masterful soul winner! He had boldness and he had tact, but, above all, he had a love for Christ and a deep gratitude for his own salvation. This man led hundreds to Christ.

In my pastorate, we had a man working for us who was timid, reticent, quiet, but, oh, what a winner of souls! Sunday after Sunday he brought people forward in the services.

Launch out into the deep! Begin now to speak of your faith in Christ, your love for Christ. Tell others how He saved you. Tell them of the joy of walking with the Lord. Let others hear of the blessedness of being a Christian.

Don't be ashamed of your Christ! Don't be embarrassed to speak of Him.

If I should die before He comes, I am 'absent from the body and present with the Lord.' What a beautiful thought! What blessed assurance!

4

The
Fighting
Heart

"I therefore so run, not as uncertainly; so fight I, not as one that beateth the air:

"But I keep under my body, and bring it into subjection: lest that by any means, when I have preached to others, I myself should be a castaway."—I Cor. 9:26, 27.

"Finally, my brethren, be strong in the Lord, and in the power of his might.

"Put on the whole armour of God, that ye may be able to stand against the wiles of the devil."—Eph. 6:10, 11.

"I have fought a good fight, I have finished my course, I have kept the faith."—II Tim. 4:7.

Moses had a fighting heart. He fought all Egypt to bring his people out of captivity. In the desert country he fought every obstacle for forty years so as to bring the people into Canaan land.

Joshua had a fighting heart. He had to follow the great Moses. The battles were tremendous, but he fought with courage.

Gideon had a fighting heart. Terrified and timid, he fought on.

Elijah had a fighting heart. He stood before the people and

declared to Israel, "How long halt ye between two opinions? if the Lord be God, follow him: but if Baal, then follow him" (I Kings 18:21).

Jeremiah had a fighting heart. The weeping prophet shed tears, but he would not stop fighting. His courage lives on to encourage each of us.

Paul had a fighting heart. With opposition from every side, he fought on. Listen to him as he wrote to young Timothy: "Fight the good fight of faith, lay hold on eternal life, whereunto thou art also called, and hast professed a good profession before many witnesses" (I Tim. 6:12).

God wants all of us to have fighting hearts—the young, the old, the timid, the bold.

The fighting heart keeps one going when all else fails. A young man in training for missions lost his wife and daughter in a car accident. He called his pastor at 3:00 a.m. to tell him what had happened. His heart was crushed, but he said to the pastor, "I'm going on to the mission field. Nothing can stop me."

The fighting heart keeps one moving forward despite dire circumstances.

The fighting heart keeps one moving forward when all is lost—job, friends, yes, even family.

The fighting heart keeps one moving forward when people declare it can't be done.

Having the fighting heart is more than being submissive to the will of God. It is more than orthodoxy, more than having compassion, more than being fundamental in your beliefs. The fighting heart stands against evil and for righteousness.

To have a fighting heart, certain things are necessary.

I. THE HEART MUST BE RIGHT WITH GOD

By repentance and faith, we come into a right relationship with our Heavenly Father. Christ is our Saviour; we are members of the family of God; we are indwelt by the Holy Spirit. Now we are ready to fight for righteousness.

Not only must the heart be right with God, but it must be kept right. Confess sin quickly (I John 1:9). Clean and dedicated, we are ready for service. Be sensitive to the needs of others. See a lost world and reach out to bring that world to salvation.

I repeat: we must have a clean heart. "Create in me a clean heart" should be our daily cry.

II. THE FIGHTING HEART SPEAKS OF FAITH

Think at once of the faith of Abraham, Moses, Joshua, Elijah, Elisha, Isaiah and Jeremiah. Think of the faith of all those named in Hebrews 11—men and women who believed God and trusted Him for every need.

Faith brings us into the family of God. "Sirs, what must I do to be saved?" The answer: "Believe on the Lord Jesus Christ, and thou shalt be saved, and thy house" (Acts 16:30, 31).

After salvation by faith, press on. Every day, faith must be a part of your life. And it must be fresh and vibrant. Faith helps us trust in times of weakness. It encourages us in times of danger.

The man was seated in the second row of the auditorium, listening intently to the message and taking notes. When the service was over, he closed his Bible and placed it on the seat. Then he walked over to the side of the building, opened a door, took out a carpet sweeper, broom and some cloths. He dusted off the pulpit stand and communion table, plugged in the carpet sweeper and began working on the floor.

This was a well-dressed man. I asked the pastor who the gentleman was who was cleaning up. He replied, "The janitor."

I said, "Yes, I can see that, but it is interesting to see a man sitting on the second row of the church taking such an interest in the Word of God, then rising and beginning his work of cleaning up."

The pastor asked, "Did you look at him carefully?"

"Yes, I believe I did."

"Then look again."

I did and noticed that the left arm was gone and the empty coat sleeve was hanging by his side.

"Pastor, do you mean to tell me that a one-armed man keeps this church clean?"

"Yes, and it is the cleanest church in America." Then the pastor told me this story.

Some years ago this man had gone overseas as a soldier for this country. His left arm was shot away. He went to the hospital and, during recovery, a man came to his bedside, told him of Christ and led him to the Saviour. When he recovered, he came back to America, came to the church and said, "Pastor, I'm a saved man. Through my serious injury and the loss of my arm, I came to Christ. Now I want to serve Him the rest of my days. Do you have a job for me?"

The pastor replied, "I have nothing to offer anyone except to be a janitor of the church."

The man answered, "I'll take the job and do my best but with one requirement: I will take not one penny of pay."

Then the pastor told me that for years this man had been keeping the church perfectly clean. He worked at his job night and day, studied his Bible, was a faithful soul winner and a man of great faith!

The fighting heart speaks of a man of faith.

III. THE FIGHTING HEART SPEAKS OF COURAGE

When God commissioned Joshua to take the place of Moses, He said to him, "Only be thou strong and very courageous, that thou mayest observe to do according to all the law, which Moses my servant commanded thee: turn not from it to the right hand or to the left, that thou mayest prosper whithersoever thou goest" (Josh. 1:7).

The Lord Jesus was forever encouraging people, "Fear not."

Twelve spies were sent out to check on the possibility of entering into Canaan. Ten came back and said it couldn't be done. Only Joshua and Caleb had faith to believe that God would give them the land.

The business world, the educational world, the domestic world, the social world—all require courage. Every individual act of life takes courage.

Wicked hearts, weak hearts, deceptive hearts will fade away, but the fighting heart goes forward courageously.

IV. THE FIGHTING HEART SPEAKS OF DETERMINATION

Men who quit are found everywhere—many like Demas, of whom Paul said, "For Demas hath forsaken me, having loved this present world."

The work of our Saviour must have determined men—men like the Apostle Paul who said, "Brethren, I count not myself to have apprehended: but this one thing I do, forgetting those things which are behind, and reaching forth unto those things which are before, I press toward the mark for the prize of the high calling of God in Christ Jesus" (Phil. 3:13, 14).

You don't have to be brilliant, but you have to be determined. The Christian with a regenerated heart will have that determination which will enable him to accomplish great things for God.

I can think of famous people who are noted for their determination. Such a one was Abraham Lincoln. Such a one was Caruso. Such a one was Michelangelo. Such a one was Franklin Delano Roosevelt. But I prefer to think of everyday people who manifested such determination that their lives were outstanding.

Years ago I heard Dr. Chester Swor, an English teacher at a college in Mississippi. I never saw a body so twisted and deformed. Infantile paralysis had touched his body, but his mind and heart were fighting. He had a Ph.D. degree and became a teacher in a college; then he went to the platform as a preacher of great power. I heard him speak many times, and he stirred my heart.

I think of another ordinary man of great determination, a deacon in a church that I pastored in Alabama, and one devoted to the Lord. In the 30's the Depression came. People lost their homes, their bank accounts, their businesses. Mr. Letcher lost everything and was left with a heavy debt.

He determined to pay off every bill that he owed. As his pastor for five years, I watched him. He was an example in faithfulness and honesty. While others took bankruptcy, he refused to do so, saying, "I will pay every bill."

After five years in the Alabama church, I came to Chattanooga.

Years went by; then one day, at the close of the service, a man walked up to me. It was Mr. Letcher. He said, "I made the trip here to tell you that I finished paying every bill that I owed. At the same time, I have continued my practice of tithing."

Such determination!

V. THE FIGHTING HEART SPEAKS OF DEVOTION

I think of that beautiful, touching scene in John 21 where the Lord questioned Simon Peter, "Lovest thou me more than these?"

How much do you love the Lord? How much do you love the work of Christ? How much do you love the souls for whom He died? Let your love for Christ give you the fighting heart.

My heart has been stirred many times by mothers I have seen who have such a devotion to their children. For example, when I came to Chattanooga, I received a phone call saying that a young man had passed away and the mother wanted me to conduct the funeral. I went to the funeral home and into the funeral parlor. When I saw the casket of a baby, I said, "You made a mistake. I am here to conduct the funeral of a young man in his teens." The undertaker said, "We have made no mistake. This is the one."

I conducted that funeral. As I talked to the mother, she told me of the years she had tended to her child. He had never grown and developed as a normal child, but she never forsook him.

I thought of another mother in Richmond, Virginia. I was having lunch one day in a beautiful home where the Christian mother had fixed up a plate and had arisen to go out of the room. "Would you like to come with me?" she asked.

I went with her to the back of the house; and lying on the bed in a lovely room was a young man about thirty, helpless, deformed, and of a simple mind. Through all the years that mother had cared for her boy. Devotion did that.

While I was preaching on the little island of Anguilla of the West Indies, a missionary took me into a little home of just one room, with little furniture. At the side of one wall of that room was a baby bed and a baby lying in it—maybe twelve or fifteen years of age, but still a baby. The black mother had cared for that child through all the years. She didn't ask for any sympathy; she just did her work. That was a picture of love.

Devotion to Christ keeps us moving forward. Devotion to Christ makes us faithful in church attendance. Devotion to Christ keeps us tithing. Devotion to Christ keeps us witnessing to loved ones and friends.

When I go to preach, sometimes I tell Him, "Lord, I am going to try again. I want to win some soul to Thee, stir some lethargic Christian to do a better job."

I have preached almost sixty-five years literally to multitudes, but I still go. Why? Because of my devotion to Him! He has saved me, called me, protected me and given me peace. Could I do less than my best?

5

The Sweetest Scene in the World

"Behold, I shew you a mystery; We shall not all sleep, but we shall all be changed."—I Cor. 15:51.

"For the Lord himself shall descend from heaven with a shout, with the voice of the archangel, and with the trump of God: and the dead in Christ shall rise first:

"Then we which are alive and remain shall be caught up together with them in the clouds, to meet the Lord in the air: and so shall we ever be with the Lord.

"Wherefore comfort one another with these words."—I Thess. 4:16–18.

Some people might question: What is the sweetest scene in the world?

A scene, a happening at the Atlanta airport, seemed mighty sweet. Mother, father and sister were waiting at the gate for the plane to bring back to them their loved one. According to their conversation, he had been away in the service for many months. They talked excitedly. They watched nervously for the plane. It finally arrived, and one of the first persons up the steps and into the waiting room was a fine-looking soldier boy. He grabbed his mother and kissed her, then his dad, and finally his sister. They stood there crying. Yes, it was a sweet scene.

But today we consider another "second coming superlative"— the sweetest scene in the world. I have no doubt in my mind but that the scene is the rapture—the time when Christ will snatch away His own, the time when the dead in Christ will be raised, the living changed, and together we will be caught up into the air to meet our blessed Lord.

Let me outline the message for you.

I. THE RETURN

1. *Christ said that He would return.* This is given to us many times in the Gospels. But I prefer to call your attention to one of the best known portions of the Word of God—John 14:1-6. The Saviour spoke of Heaven, and in the midst of this He said, "...I will come again, and receive you unto myself; that where I am, there ye may be also." I do not need any other word than this simple word of our Saviour, "I will come again."

2. *Two heavenly beings also spoke of His return.* On the day of the ascension, as the disciples watched Christ go out of their sight, two men in white apparel called unto them and said, "Ye men of Galilee, why stand ye gazing up into heaven? this same Jesus, which is taken up from you into heaven, shall so come in like manner as ye have seen him go into heaven" (Acts 1:11).

It is plainly evident from the Scriptures that God sent two angels to stand and speak to the sorrowing disciples. As a consequence, the disciples went back into Jerusalem and "were continually in the temple, praising and blessing God."

3. *Paul said that Christ would return.* This is given in many portions of the writings of the apostle, but I call your attention to the verse that I read a moment ago in I Thessalonians 4:16, "For the Lord himself shall descend from heaven with a shout, with the voice of the archangel, and with the trump of God: and the dead in Christ shall rise first."

4. *Peter spoke of the return of Christ.* Second Peter 3 gives the answer of the apostle to the scoffers who were saying, "Where is the promise of his coming?" The apostle went on to give some reasons for the delay in the coming of Christ: "The Lord is not slack concerning his promise, as some men count slackness; but is longsuffering to us-ward, not willing that any should perish, but that all should come to repentance."

5. *John spoke of the return of Christ when the Spirit of the Lord inspired him to write the Revelation.* In the first chapter we find these words, "Behold, he cometh with clouds; and every eye shall see him, and they also which pierced him: and all kindreds of the earth shall wail because of him."

In the very closing of this momentous book, we find John writing, "He which testifieth these things saith, Surely I come quickly. Amen. Even so, come, Lord Jesus."

Two things we should remember about the coming of our Saviour:

(1) The time of His return is indefinite: "Watch therefore: for ye know not what hour your Lord doth come" (Matt. 24:42). This eliminates all time-setting. We simply know that Christ is coming again, and we ought be ready for His coming at any time.

(2) His coming is imminent—that is, it may be at any moment. His coming is like a sword hanging by a thread: at any second the God in Heaven may speak the word, and Christ will come again. He said Himself, "Therefore be ye also ready: for in such an hour as ye think not the Son of man cometh."

II. THE RESURRECTION

At His coming the dead in Christ shall be raised first. The return of the Saviour and the resurrection of the saints are bound together. At His voice the dead will arise. ". . . and the dead in Christ shall rise first" (I Thess. 4:16). Then we read, "In a moment, in the twinkling of an eye, at the last trump: for the trumpet shall sound, and the dead shall be raised incorruptible, and we shall be changed" (I Cor. 15:52).

The resurrection means the following:

1. *Victory over death* is promised us in every word of Christ. Jesus said, "He that hath the Son hath life; and he that hath not the Son of God hath not life."

2. *The resurrection means victory over the grave.* "It is appointed unto men once to die." The grave is the portion of all men. The grave is dark and somber, but in Christ there is victory.

3. *Resurrection means victory over the mystery of death.* No one can understand why one person dies and another lives. We do not know why one dies young and another lives to an old age. But this we can know: at the resurrection, we will understand the mystery of death.

Write down this fact: Christ is coming again; and when He comes, the dead in Christ shall be raised. The resurrection bodies will be given to the saints who have gone before.

These resurrection bodies will not be subject to sickness or death.

In Revelation 21:3, 4, we find the state of the saints in the millennial period:

"And I heard a great voice out of heaven saying, Behold, the tabernacle of God is with men, and he will dwell with them, and they shall be his people, and God himself shall be with them, and be their God.

"And God shall wipe away all tears from their eyes; and there shall be no more death, neither sorrow, nor crying, neither shall there be any more pain: for the former things are passed away."

4. *The resurrection body is eternal.* It cannot be injured by accident or enemy nor affected by seasons or events.

5. *The resurrection body will not know limitations and deficiencies.* Every limitation, every defect is to be left in the grave. The body sown in corruption is to be raised in incorruption. The one sown in weakness is to be raised in strength. The one sown in dishonor is to be raised in glory. The one sown a natural body is to be raised a spiritual body.

I need not endeavor to draw a picture of the condition of people as they are in this day. How weak, how frail, how pain-filled are our bodies! But one day they shall be like the Saviour's.

Our wheelchair singer, Mrs. Georgia Webb Gentry, suffered so much in a body that longed to live, yet was bound to die. For many years she was unable to walk alone. She loved to sing, but her voice changed in timber and quality as sickness laid hold upon her. But one day the wheelchair singer will have a body complete, entire—a body that will not change through all the endless ages.

Christ is coming again. There will be a great resurrection—the resurrection of the saved. "This is the first resurrection."

III. THE RAPTURE

"For this we say unto you by the word of the Lord, that we which are alive and remain unto the coming of the Lord shall not prevent them which are asleep. . . .

"Then we which are alive and remain shall be caught up together with them in the clouds, to meet the Lord in the air: and so shall we ever be with the Lord."—I Thess. 4:15, 17.

1. *At the coming of Jesus there will be a rewedding of body and spirit.* ". . . even so them also which sleep in Jesus will God bring with him." The dead in Christ are now with the Lord; but at His shout the bodies of the saved will be raised, and body and spirit will be joined together.

2. *The living will be changed, in a moment, in the twinkling of an eye.* In writing to the church in Corinth, Paul said, "Behold, I shew you a mystery; We shall not all sleep, but we shall all be changed" (I Cor. 15:51).

3. *We shall ever be with the Lord.* The dead are raised, the living are changed, and together we are caught up into the air to meet our Saviour. How blessed is the thought! How we should rejoice in this glorious fact!

My heart goes out to the poor, fumbling religionists of this day. The noted British historian, Dr. Arnold Toynbee, made a visit to our city. He went from here to other universities. In one of his lectures he discussed the future of Christians, Jews, and four other religions. He said:

> The high religions each claim that they have the sole reve-
> lation of truth and the sole means of salvation. This claim

cannot be made convincingly by any of the religions because they are all based on the same foundation—direct revelation from God.

According to the papers, Dr. Toynbee said that religions would have to make three changes:

> If they hope to come back to the positions they held before the 17th Century, they must learn to work together, keep up with the social questions of the day, and most importantly, reconsider their doctrines.

I prefer not to make any lengthy comment about Dr. Toynbee. I have only pity for a man who does not know Christ. But I do want to say this: it is not necessary for a person to be highly educated, sophisticated, learned according to the world, to understand plain English.

When Jesus said, "I will come again," no one can change doctrine like this. It is so plain, so apparent, so evident that it must be received. You cannot change what Paul said about the second coming of Christ: "For the Lord himself shall descend from heaven with a shout, with the voice of the archangel, and with the trump of God: and the dead in Christ shall rise first." Every child here can understand that.

IV. THE REJOICING

"We shall all be changed" (I Cor. 15:51); *". . . and so shall we ever be with the Lord"* (I Thess. 4:17).

Rejoice? Yes! Rejoice now in the fact that He is coming again. And rejoice forever and forever when we stand in His presence.

1. *His coming means release*—release from weaknesses and fears. We are going to be changed—we are going to be made like Him—we shall see Him as He is: "Beloved, now are we the sons of God, and it doth not yet appear what we shall be: but we know that, when he shall appear, we shall be like him; for we shall see him as he is" (I John 3:2).

Released from this weak body, from sickness, from wrecks, from afflictions, from age! Many people are crying for release from their sufferings, but only can the Christian desire release hopefully. He knows that in Christ there is a blessed future.

But maybe I had better encourage you some in the matter of living day by day. The future holds much for us, but live today. Dwight L. Moody once saw at a clock shop a pendulum which was waiting to be fixed on a new timepiece he was purchasing. He said:

> I began to calculate how long it would be before the big wheels of the instrument were worn out and its work done. The clock would be expected to tick night and day, so many times a minute, sixty times that much every hour, twenty-four times that much every day, and three hundred sixty-five times that much every year.
>
> The more I thought of it, the more it staggered me. It was awful! What a row of figures it made! Millions of ticks. I thought I could hear the poor pendulum exclaim, "I can never do it!" But I imagined the clockmaker saying, "Oh, yes, you can. You need only do one tick at a time. You can do that, can't you?"
>
> "Oh, yes," the pendulum replied.
>
> "Well," said the clockmaker, "that is all that will be expected of you."
>
> So the pendulum went to work steadily, ticking one tick at a time; and years later, now, that clock is still ticking quite cheerfully.

Your life may seem exceedingly hard today, but bear it one day at a time. Whatever troubles may be yours, simply take them, knowing that one day you will have release.

2. *When He comes, there will be a reunion.* The dead in Christ will be raised, the living will be changed, and we will be caught up together in the clouds.

3. *His coming will mean rejoicing.* Oh, what rejoicing will be ours when we stand in His presence!

"The Vail of Tears" pictures a dreary, night-shadowed land of rocks and precipices. In the center of the dismal scene is a deep ravine. Down along this rough way, the Lord is seen tenderly advancing toward a weeping crowd, bearing on His left shoulder a blood-stained cross while His right hand is stretched out in loving sympathy and invitation to the sorrowful assembly. His eye, tender with pitying love, seems to be saying, "Come unto me, all ye that labour and are heavy laden." Some exhausted ones are seen kneeling at His feet while others, still looking for His heavenly comfort, are fleeing to His open arms.

Way down in the shadow of the painting, almost concealed amid the dark shadows, is the ugly, writhing form of a huge serpent, clinging with its thick coils to a blasted tree. It is symbolic of the fact that the valley of weeping is due to the curse of sin.

Apparently the artist sought to proclaim to the world the wondrous story that those who come to Christ find certain comfort and need "fear no evil," though they walk through the awesome valley of the shadow of death.

The picture is a good one, but here is a better one. We are coming to the time of no tears. We are coming into the presence of our Saviour, and we shall be with Him forever and forever.

> Oh, my soul, be not weary and troubled,
>   For God is still on the throne.
> Though the storms of adversity gather,
>   Remember, He strengthens His own.
> Though the lightning around you be flashing
>   And the billowing waves o'er you roll,
> There is peace in the midst of the tempest;
>   There is peace, so be still, oh, my soul!
>
> Oh, my soul, be not sad nor discouraged,
>   For God is still on the throne.
> Though the pathway of life may be rugged,
>   Remember, you walk not alone.
> The Saviour is with you each moment,
>   To lead you on mountain or knoll.
> There is peace in the valley or summit;
>   There is peace, so be still, oh, my soul.
>
> Oh, my soul, do not shrink from affliction,
>   For God is still on the throne;
> Remember the suffering on Calvary
>   And the agony borne all alone.
> Though the lengthening shadows of weakness
>   Steep the body in pain's dread control,
> There is peace in the midnight of suffering;
>   There is peace, so be still, oh, my soul.

Oh, my soul, do not weary of waiting,
    For God is still on the throne;
Remember, His promised appearing
    Will gladden the hearts of His own.
Tho' He linger a little while longer,
    His praises for man to extol,
There is peace, for His coming is nearer,
    There is peace, so be still, oh, my soul.

In the light of all that I have given you, listen to the three exhortations coming from the apostle. He said we are to *watch*, for "the day of the Lord so cometh as a thief in the night." He said we are to *wake up*: "Therefore let us not sleep, as do others; but let us watch and be sober." And he exhorts us to *work* and to live for Christ. In I Thessalonians 5:16–22 are the pungent exhortations of the apostle to faithfulness.

My friend, Christ is coming. Are you ready? Do you know Him as your Saviour? Are you living for Him daily?

6

Voices! Voices! Voices!

"Now the Lord had said unto Abram, Get thee out of thy country, and from thy kindred, and from thy father's house, unto a land that I will show thee:

"And I will make of thee a great nation, and I will bless thee, and make thy name great; and thou shalt be a blessing:

"And I will bless them that bless thee, and curse him that curseth thee: and in thee shall all families of the earth be blessed."—Gen. 12:1–3.

"There are, it may be, so many kinds of voices in the world, and none of them is without signification."—I Cor. 14:10.

"For he received from God the Father honor and glory, when there came such a voice to him from the excellent glory, This is my beloved Son, in whom I am well pleased."—II Pet. 1:17.

When I was eighteen, I took my first voice lesson. Because of my loud singing in a Sunday school class, Rev. J. N. Binford, my pastor, asked me to lead the singing in Cedar Creek Baptist Church.

I thought I had reached the peak of human attainment, being the song leader of Cedar Creek Baptist Church! My pride knew no bounds. (Of course, it never occurred to me that they asked me because they could find no one else!)

But then, I "suppose" I must have lacked something, for a friend of mine suggested that I ought to take voice lessons.

Voice lessons? My dad was mystified. He couldn't carry a tune and knew nothing at all about singing. He asked me, "What in the world are voice lessons?"

I was recommended to a teacher in Louisville named Mr. Shearer. He accepted me. He was a German and gave emphasis to breath control. (On my first lesson my exhalation was thirty-one seconds; in a few months I exceeded four minutes.)

Later I studied with William Layne Vick of Memphis, and later with John Sample in Chicago. (Nine dollars per lesson in Depression days; I lived on sixty cents per day.)

When a sophomore in the University of Louisville, I was soloist of the university choir, sang on WHAS, WLAP and later on WMC, Memphis, and WSM, Nashville.

I began to admire the great voices of the world—John Charles Thomas, James Melton, Norman Cordon, Lawrence Tibbett. In concert I heard Lily Pons, Grace Moore and many others.

Voices were attractive to me and still are. *Voices! Voices! Voices!*

In our missionary conference I listened to our speakers and watched the thousands of young people as they listened. Voices!

Some listened and responded.

Some listened and delayed any response.

Some paid no attention to any voice or any message.

At a special occasion, I spoke in a Sunday morning service at a good church. Many guests were there. To my left on the second row were seated six or eight people—the owners of large hotels and motels in the neighborhood. On my right were seated eight or ten politicians running for office: a senator, a representative, a tax assessor, etc. They all came by invitation from the pastor.

What did they hear? Did they allow God's voice to penetrate their minds? Were they capable of hearing? Were they regenerated people? Could they hear the voice of God?

We are thinking about voices.

1. *The voice of God.* This Bible is the voice of God. God speaks! He spoke to Moses. He spoke to Isaiah. Never neglect your Bible. It is God speaking to you.

2. *The voice of the Son.* Christ speaks! Saul of Tarsus discovered this. In Acts 9:5 Christ said, "I am Jesus whom thou persecutest...."

3. *The voice of the Holy Spirit.* The Holy Spirit speaks! "The Holy Ghost said, Separate me Barnabas and Saul for the work whereunto I have called them." The Holy Spirit speaks now to us. He indwells us.

But there are other voices.

1. *The voice of the world.* Demas heard that voice and forsook Paul. "For Demas hath forsaken me, having loved this present world..." (II Tim. 4:10). Many young people hear the voice of the world. The world is attractive and offers much to youth; yes, to all ages: money, fame, popularity.

2. *The voice of the flesh.* Poor old Solomon, the wisest and the richest man in the world, was led away by the flesh. (See I Kings 11:1-8.) Television, styles and books appeal to the flesh.

3. *The voice of Satan.* King Saul heard that voice and followed it. The Devil spoke and tempted Christ and failed. Incessantly these voices speak, and many follow from youth on up. From Genesis 1:3 where God said, "Let there be light: and there was light," to Revelation 22:20 where Christ says, "Surely I come quickly. Amen," God speaks!

Out of the maze of voices in this world, we must hear the voice of God. Don't listen to the sinful and selfish voices of the world, the flesh and the Devil.

Some negative advice:

Don't listen to the wrong voices. Had I done so, then Camp Joy, Tennessee Temple University, and Worldwide Faith Missions would never have existed. When I was called to preach, some voices called me foolish.

Don't listen to wicked voices. Profane, suggestive, evil, wicked voices speak by radio, television, newspapers, and billboards. Shut them out. Turn them off.

Don't listen to deceptive voices. The world is filled with satanic deceivers. A man who lost all he had said, "I was deceived." Youth is also being deceived today!

Don't listen to cheap, selfish voices. "Self" is the theme of the world.

God is forgotten. Cheap advice is taken. Paul fought self! "So fight I, not as one that beateth the air: But I keep under my body, and bring it into subjection: lest that by any means, when I have preached to others, I myself should be a castaway" (I Cor. 9:26, 27).

I. THE VOICE WE MUST HEAR
IS THE VOICE OF GOD

1. *He speaks by His Word.* Read it to let Him speak to you!

Don't read it to get an award. Don't read it to make a name. Don't read it just to memorize it. Read it so God can speak to you!

David said, "Thy word have I hid in mine heart, that I might not sin against thee" (Ps. 119:11).

His *Word* will keep you from sin, guide you into right living, and direct you into service.

2. *He speaks by His servants who use the Word.* How much we owe to great preachers of the Word!

I listened to H. A. Ironside at Moody Church in 1934.

I was living in Chicago on sixty cents per day. Lonely, discouraged and perplexed, the Word given then by His servant helped me!

How much I owe to J. N. Binford, L. W. Benedict, R. G. Lee, George Truett, Frank Norris, Mordecai Ham, W. B. Riley and many others.

3. *He speaks through the indwelling Holy Spirit.* I have no one else to help me! The Word is before me; the Holy Spirit is in me to direct me. A Christian can hear the voice of God!

II. THE VOICE THAT NEVER FAILS

The Bible records the failures of man. Secular history tells of man's failures. But God never fails!

> **Jesus never fails,**
> **Jesus never fails;**
> **Heaven and earth may pass away,**
> **But Jesus never fails.**

1. *God's voice gives words of encouragement.* Read the Psalms! Read Romans 8:28. Unfailingly, He speaks encouragement.

My good friend Bill did not listen. He preached in the First

Baptist Church of Nashville, then committed suicide. He did not hear God's voice!

2. *God's voice gives words of strength:* "But they that wait upon the Lord shall renew their strength; they shall mount up with wings as eagles; they shall run, and not be weary; and they shall walk, and not faint" (Isa. 40:31).

In times of weakness, "wait" for God to speak to you and strengthen you.

3. *God's voice gives words of life.* Salvation! He never fails when men hear His Word. "So then faith cometh by hearing, and hearing by the word of God" (Rom. 10:17).

III. THE VOICE THAT OFFERS WHAT I NEED

Man is weak and needy.

1. *Hear His voice in the hour of discouragement.* Satan's master tricks: *doubt* and *discouragement.* Don't be tricked! "Lest Satan should get an advantage of us: for we are not ignorant of his devices" (II Cor. 2:11).

In an hour of doubt and discouragement, Dr. Weigle wrote his song:

> **No one ever cared for me like Jesus,**
> **There's no other friend so kind as He;**
> **No one else could take the sin and darkness from me,**
> **O how much He cared for me.**

2. *Hear that voice in times of temptation.* "There hath no temptation taken you but such as is common to man: but God is faithful, who will not suffer you to be tempted above that ye are able; but will with the temptation also make a way to escape, that ye may be able to bear it" (I Cor. 10:13).

Hear Him young and old! When tempted to quit, when tempted to sin, when tempted to laugh at standards, run to Him. Listen to His voice.

3. *Hear His voice in times of darkness.* He cares. Satan will speak, but refuse to hear him! Go to God when you lose a loved one! Hear Him when the message comes! Hear Him at the side of the casket!

Hear Him at the grave! Psalm 23:1 tells us, "The Lord is my shepherd; I shall not want."

4. *Hear His voice in the time of failure.*

Joshua 7 tells of Joshua's failure in Ai. God told him his trouble, then sent him on!

Paul failed at Lystra. His enemies stoned him and left him for dead; but Paul rose up and went on! Yes, hear His voice in failure!

5. *Hear His voice for direction.* God directed Abraham, Moses, Joshua, Elijah, and Daniel.

Yesterday a young man said, "I have three ways I can go. How do I know which way?" I advised him to wait and pray for direction. Since He directed others, He will direct us! Place yourself before Him and say, "Take me, Lord."

I close with this illustration:

A nice lady said to a pastor at Cadle Tabernacle in Indianapolis, Indiana,

> I'm glad you are concerned about youth. When my brother got in trouble, everybody turned against him.
>
> John went to Sunday school a few Sundays. Then he quit. Nobody cared. He went to a revival in the old country church. At the invitation, he went forward and knelt at the altar; but no one spoke to him.
>
> He arose, went to the back of the church and declared, "I'll never go to church again."
>
> He didn't. My brother was John Dillinger, Public Enemy Number One, killer and gangster.

7

The Highest Test
Ever Presented
to Man

"But why dost thou judge thy brother? or why dost thou set at nought thy brother? for we shall all stand before the judgment seat of Christ.

"For it is written, As I live, saith the Lord, every knee shall bow to me, and every tongue shall confess to God.

"So then every one of us shall give account of himself to God."
—Rom. 14:10–12.

"For other foundation can no man lay than that is laid, which is Jesus Christ.

"Now if any man build upon this foundation gold, silver, precious stones, wood, hay, stubble;

"Every man's work shall be made manifest: for the day shall declare it, because it shall be revealed by fire; and the fire shall try every man's work of what sort it is.

"If any man's work abide which he hath built thereupon, he shall receive a reward.

"If any man's work shall be burned, he shall suffer loss: but he himself shall be saved; yet so as by fire."—I Cor. 3:11–15.

"For we must all appear before the judgment seat of Christ; that

every one may receive the things done in his body, according to that he hath done, whether it be good or bad."—II Cor. 5:10.

The happiest message might be summarized in the word given by Jesus to Zacchaeus: "For the Son of man is come to seek and to save that which was lost" (Luke 19:10).

The Apostle Paul summed it up in writing to the church in Corinth: "For I delivered unto you first of all that which I also received, how that Christ died for our sins according to the Scriptures" (I Cor. 15:3).

The greatest event in the world was the death of Jesus Christ. The greatest message in the world was salvation through the shed blood of the crucified, buried and risen Saviour.

With these facts in mind, the greatest event of the future is the second coming of Jesus Christ. The Bible speaks repeatedly of that coming. It is mentioned more than three hundred times. In his epistles, Paul alone refers to it at least fifty times. Every time we come to the Lord's table, we are showing "the Lord's death till he come."

The coming of Christ will be a time of reward for the faithful. It will also be a time of reunion. With the coming of Christ, there will be a first resurrection. The dead in Christ will be raised, the living changed, and together we shall be caught up into the air to meet our Lord.

This past week as I stood by the graveside of one of our faithful members, I thought of the resurrection day and what it will mean for Christ to come and the dead in Christ to be raised first. I thought of the resurrection bodies—bodies made like that of our Saviour.

Dr. Len G. Broughton, famous preacher of Atlanta, Georgia, and Spurgeon's Tabernacle, used to tell of an old judge in the mountains of Georgia. The judge was somewhat ignorant of the law but abundant in common sense.

Coming into court one morning he saw a witness seated in the witness chair with a shawl around him. He asked, "You here to bear testimony?"

"Yes."

The judge said, "Put up your right hand."

The witness said, "Judge, my right hand is paralyzed."

"Hold up your left hand then," said the judge.

"Judge, the left arm is off."

In a spirit of semi-exasperation, the judge shouted, "Then stick up your foot!"

The man answered, "Sir, I got them both shot off in the last war."

The old judge said, "Then stand on your head—you've got to put up something in this court!"

Ah, listen! One day Jesus will come to receive His own. Then we shall have bodies made like that of our Saviour. What a day of reunion, what a day of rejoicing that will be!

His coming will also be a time of reigning. Paul said, "If we suffer, we shall also reign with him."

But in this message, I will speak on the judgments, particularly on the judgment seat of Christ.

The Bible specifically gives us the story of three judgments to come. *(1) The judgment seat of Christ.* (We have already read Scripture portions relating to this judgment, and we shall say more about it in a moment.) *(2) The judgment of living nations.* This judgment takes place at the revelation of Christ. This is when all nations will be gathered before the Lord and "he shall separate them one from another, as a shepherd divideth his sheep from the goats." *(3) There will be the great white throne judgment,* recorded in Revelation 20:11-15. The lost dead, small and great, will be brought before God; and the books will be opened.

But now, let your mind settle upon the judgment seat of Christ. When does it take place? At the return of Christ for His saints. "And, behold, I come quickly; and my reward is with me, to give every man according as his work shall be."

And also II Timothy 4:8: "Henceforth there is laid up for me a crown of righteousness, which the Lord, the righteous judge, shall give me at that day: and not to me only, but unto all them also that love his appearing."

The judgment seat of Christ will take place when the dead in Christ are raised and the living are changed and caught up into the air to meet the Lord. At this time we will be judged for our works and service.

With this as an introduction, let me give the following outline.

I. THE EXACT JUDGMENT

Why do I say this? Because Christ will be the Judge. There will be no exceptions, no lying, no buying of favors. Christ, the eternal Son of God, will be the Judge of His own followers.

In this day many are registering doubts in their positions on Christ. Many religions are arising throughout the country which deny the virgin birth of Jesus, His physical resurrection from the grave, His ascension to the right hand of God. Men are trying to reduce Christ to the level of mortal man. I have books by present-day authors denying the deity of Christ.

Who will be the judge? Christ, the sinner's substitute. How can men turn away from the Lord of whom it was said, "But he was wounded for our transgressions, he was bruised for our iniquities: the chastisement of our peace was upon him; and with his stripes we are healed" (Isa. 53:5)?

Yes, we shall all stand before the judgment seat of Christ, there to give an account of ourselves to God. It will be an exact judgment, conducted by a holy Saviour.

II. THE IGNORED JUDGMENT

We do not expect lost sinners to know anything about it; but the sad thing is, the majority of professing Christians know little about this coming judgment.

World leaders know nothing about it.

If you should call the President of the United States, a Baptist, and say, "Sir, tell me what you know about the judgment seat of Christ," what do you suppose he would say?

If you should call upon the pope to give a summary of the teaching of the judgment seat, what would be his response? If you should ask the prime minister of England to give his ideas on the judgment seat, what do you think would be his answer? Most people who profess to know Christ know nothing about this judgment or, at least, know very little.

Perhaps we should also say that most people want to know nothing about such a judgment. Why? They prefer to live their own way. They prefer to believe some of the erroneous ideas of the past, such as one general judgment.

I say the judgment has been ignored by civic leaders, church leaders, professional people, and the man on the street.

Ah, but wait! Way back in the hills of Tennessee there is a little country church holding a service right now. The preacher is standing to give his message on "The Judgment Seat of Christ."

Perhaps he never went beyond the third grade, but he knows this truth, and he is giving it to his people. Where does he find it? The same Bible that tells of redeeming love and of salvation through faith in Christ, tells of the judgment seat of Christ, a judgment ignored by most people.

III. THE SURPRISING JUDGMENT

Christians are at this judgment. Paul wrote to the church at Rome, "For we shall all stand before the judgment seat of Christ." To the church in Corinth he said, "For we must all appear before the judgment seat of Christ; that every one many receive the things done in his body, according to that he hath done, whether it be good or bad" (II Cor. 5:10).

This judgment will be for judging works and service, not salvation. When will it happen? Just after the coming of Christ. The dead in Christ have been raised, the living have been changed, and we stand before Christ and are judged for our works and service.

Many wonderful truths should come out in this portion of the message. Maybe we can point out a few. We are judged, not for quantity but quality. "Every man's work shall be made manifest: for the day shall declare it, because it shall be revealed by fire; and the fire shall try every man's work of what sort it is" (I Cor. 3:13).

The judgment is not on how much, but what kind. For example, let us imagine a Christian standing before the judgment seat. He was prominent in his local church and chairman of every committee there. He helped to hire the preacher and helped kick him out. His works are put into the testing fires. They burn up! Hear him say, "Wait a minute, Sir. I was a leader in my church. I presided at every business meeting. I gave my money. What's wrong here? My works were good down on the earth, but up here they were wood, hay and stubble and have been burned. What's the trouble?"

The answer will be apparent as he stands before the judgment seat, apparent because he will be standing there in his resurrection or glorified body. The reply will come from the judgment seat, "...saved; yet so as by fire."

But here stands a little lady who lived in a poor section of the town, a poor woman. She came to church faithfully. She gave of her money, used her influence to help others, and was a soul winner. Many came forward in the church Sunday after Sunday because of her faithful efforts.

She is now before the Judge at the judgment seat. Her works are brought out. They are cast into the testing fires—and stand! They are made up of gold, silver and precious stones. "If any man's work abide which he hath built thereupon, he shall receive a reward."

This one, in quiet fervency of soul, won others to Christ. She never stopped through her long lifetime. She took no spiritual vacations but continued in the work God had called her to do.

Now, perhaps we should summarize this point of the message:

1. *There will be no unsaved people at this judgment.* The saved and the lost do not stand together at the same judgment. A person's salvation has been settled before he comes to this one.

2. *Our works are to be tested by fire.* In this judgment all will be judged alike, judged on the quality of work, not quantity.

3. *We know that some will receive a reward.* If a man's work abide, he is rewarded by the Lord.

4. *We know that some will suffer loss.* "If any man's work shall be burned, he shall suffer loss: but he himself shall be saved; yet so as by fire" (I Cor. 3:15). Please notice that this is a judgment of saved souls; therefore, a soul cannot be lost, just the reward.

The judgment seat need not be a surprise if you know your

Bible. You will understand that which is going to happen and will be prepared when you see the Master seated at the place of judgment. The only surprising thing might be the fact of your works. You may have thought that you had done more. Selfish works will be consumed and forgotten. Unloving works will vanish in the flames of the judgment. Spasmodic, unfaithful works will soon disappear.

IV. THE STIMULATING JUDGMENT

1. *The thought of this judgment purifies the life.*

"Beloved, now are we the sons of God, and it doth not yet appear what we shall be: but we know that, when he shall appear, we shall be like him; for we shall see him as he is.

"And every man that hath this hope in him purifieth himself, even as he is pure."—I John 3:2, 3.

If I am a sincere Christian looking for the return of Jesus Christ, then I will certainly exercise care in the way I live. If I know I am going to be judged for my works and service, then I will surely want to be ready to meet Him.

Check your life to see that it is clean and pure and undefiled as you stand before the Judge.

2. *This stimulating judgment stirs service.* I confess that I need an incentive for work; I need something to keep me busy. I must not be concerned about getting a reward here but about when I stand before Him to give an account of myself. Paul tells me that I must be "fervent in spirit; serving the Lord." The judgment seat of Christ can be a great asset in producing faithfulness.

3. *This stimulating judgment opens eyes.* Christ is coming. Be watchful. Paul tells us that the crown of righteousness will be given to those who love the appearing of our Lord. If we love Him, surely we will be watching for His coming.

Believers form the bride of Christ. Surely the bride will be looking for the return of the Bridegroom. If you were engaged and your lover said, "Sweetheart, I am going away for awhile to prepare a home, but I will come again for you," what would you do? Forget him? No!

You would be thinking of him and longing for his return. You would be thinking, *He may come this day.* Such should be the attitude of the Christian. Jesus said, "Watch therefore, for ye know neither the day nor the hour wherein the Son of man cometh."

As we close our consideration of the judgment seat of Christ and of the test that is coming to each one of us, let us think of two things: (1) Are we giving our best to Christ in service? Do we love Him enough to serve Him faithfully? (2) Are we ministering to the needs of others? We have His command, so we must not fail. Christ is coming; be ready for that hour. Be watchful. Be busy proclaiming the message of Christ and preparing for His coming back to receive us.

The late Dr. Biederwolf used to tell about a thrilling espisode out of English history. He told how a small army of English soldiers were in the garrison when it was surrounded by a band of 30,000 blood-thirsty savages crying for vengeance and filling the air with terrifying shrieks.

By some skillful maneuvering, the English managed to slip quietly away; but one of their number was left behind. When his companions stole away, he was sound asleep; and when he awoke, he found himself, to his horrible plight, held in the garrison with 30,000 ferocious, blood-thirsty savages, yelling for the sight of a white man's face and for the taste of a white man's blood.

Then he, too, managed to slip away by a secret passage. But when he caught up with his fleeing companions, they didn't know who he was. His hair had turned white with fright; and when they asked him for his name, it had gone from his mind, and he didn't know it.

I use that story to emphasize the need for preparedness, that we might be looking for the Son of man.

"Therefore be ye also ready: for in such an hour as ye think not the Son of man cometh."—Matt. 24:44.

8

Faith in the Darkest Hour

"Notwithstanding the Lord stood with me, and strengthened me; that by me the preaching might be fully known, and that all the Gentiles might hear: and I was delivered out of the mouth of the lion." — II Tim. 4:17.

This was a dark hour for Paul. He was writing to Timothy from Rome. He had doubtless appeared before Nero, the vicious, bloodthirsty king of Rome. At this appearance, all of the Christians fled from him, says II Timothy 4:16: "At my first answer no man stood with me, but all men forsook me: I pray God that it may not be laid to their charge."

Paul likened his trial before Nero to a little man before a fierce lion. The lion appeared and opened his mouth to devour him, but God intervened and he was delivered.

Paul praised God for deliverance and said, "The Lord shall deliver me from every evil work, and will preserve me unto his heavenly kingdom: to whom be glory for ever and ever."

As I read this final chapter from Paul, I am impressed by three things:

1. The youthfulness of Paul's attitude. He was not young in years, but he was youthful in attitude and interest. He addressed himself to young Timothy:

"Preach the word; be instant in season, out of season; reprove, rebuke, exhort with all longsuffering and doctrine.

"For the time will come when they will not endure sound doctrine; but after their own lusts shall they heap to themselves teachers, having itching ears;

"And they shall turn away their ears from the truth, and shall be turned unto fables."—II Tim. 4:2-4.

Yes, he said much about himself, but he also talked about others. At least sixteen people are mentioned in these last verses. Sometimes older people face a danger of talking only about themselves—about their ailments, their financial burdens, their personal problems. But not Paul! He talked about others, too. Keep a vital interest in others. Don't lose your touch with people. This will bring youthfulness.

2. *The helpfulness of his remarks.* Concerned about Timothy, he said, "I charge thee therefore before God, and the Lord Jesus Christ, who shall judge the quick and the dead at his appearing and his kingdom."

In trying to help Timothy, he mentioned that one man named Demas had forsaken him and turned back to the world. This was a kind way to relate a very painful matter. Paul was indicating that even the best of men may fail.

He mentioned also Alexander: "Alexander the coppersmith did me much evil: the Lord reward him according to his works." Then he said to Timothy, "Of whom be thou ware also; for he hath greatly withstood our words." In other words, "Timothy, watch out for this man. He will cause you trouble." Paul was warning a youth. He was concerned about others.

3. *The hopefulness of his remarks.* When others had failed, the Lord stood by him. He was never troubled about the Lord; He knew He would never fail. He was ready for death or for the appearing of Christ. "Henceforth there is laid up for me a crown of righteousness, which the Lord, the righteous judge, shall give me at that day:

and not to me only, but unto all them also that love his appearing" (II Tim. 4:8).

Paul was looking ahead. This is good for both young and old. Paul had had much suffering, but he made little mention of it. His attitude was hopeful. He was like the man who addressed his aging body thus:

> When you can go no further, I shall leave you and be free. When we separate, I shall continue to exist. A power greater than you and I started us on our journey. Your journey is approaching its end, and you are aware of it. My journey has merely begun, and I know it because I have never been more alive. Our separation is, therefore, not one of sadness but of joy. You are weary and want to stop, and I am longing to alight from this slow vehicle and go on without you.

This seems to be somewhat the thinking of Paul as he looked toward the end of life and thought of coming into the presence of the Lord. Paul enjoyed life. The wholesomeness of his words indicates this: but he was also ready for the time when he would come into the presence of God. Paul was positive, not negative.

I was reading about a mother who was quite negative in her thinking. Riding on the train with her four children, she didn't try to interest the little ones, only sought to restrain them.

Her conversation was a mere series of ejaculations: "No!" "Stop!" "Don't do that!" When one little fellow ran to the other end of the car beyond the mother's range of vision, she sent his older sister with the instruction, "Go see what Willie is doing, and tell him to stop it."

This is not the attitude of the apostle. There was hopefulness as he looked to the future.

Another outline forced itself on me as I read the chapter:

Paul's personal dilemma. Since some of his friends had turned away from his side, he felt a bit lonely.

Paul's personal danger. He had been delivered from Nero, but still he faced death.

Paul's personal deliverance. "The Lord shall deliver me," "the Lord stood with me," "the Lord...strengthened me," "I was delivered out of the mouth of the lion," "the Lord shall deliver me," "the Lord. . . will preserve me."

You can't stop a man with faith like that!

Considering the subject, "Faith in the Darkest Hour," let us look at the apostle again and think of this outline.

I. THE FOUNDATION FOR HIS FAITH

Go back to the Damascus road. Paul's faith in the living Christ actually began on the day that he watched the stoning of Stephen. No, he was not saved on that day, but on that day he saw the power of the living Son of God.

On the Damascus road, Christ met him face to face. There came a light from Heaven and a voice saying, "Saul, Saul, why persecutest thou me?" As a result of that encounter, Paul said, "Lord, what wilt thou have me to do?"

Go back to the Arabian years. He was saved on his way to Damascus; then he took to Arabia to orient himself to his new position in life. This indicates that we might be better off to stop once in awhile and adjust our own hearts and think through our situations. Quite often God has something He wants us to know; but being so busy, we don't take time to listen to Him.

Take time to hear His voice, to listen to His words, words which might well change your life.

And then as we think about the foundation for his faith, we think back over his years of preaching and witnessing. Had God ever failed him? No. Suffering? Yes. Privations? Yes. But God never failed Paul.

If you yourself are to have faith in the darkest hours, you had better get established.

1. Be sure that Christ is the foundation for your life. In writing to the church in Corinth, Paul said, "For other foundation can no man lay than that is laid, which is Jesus Christ" (I Cor. 3:11).

You aren't going to get very far until you know that Christ is your Saviour and that you are trusting Him.

2. Be established by the Word. There were no doubts in Paul's mind about God's Word, for he wrote, "All scripture is given by inspiration of God, and is profitable for doctrine, for reproof, for correction, for instruction in righteousness."

3. Be established in His work. God has a task for every child of His. He has called you to that task; now be sure you do it efficiently. Be established in the fact that every Christian is to witness.

"The Foundation for His Faith" I am emphasizing so you might have faith in your darkest hour.

II. THE FORCE OF HIS FAITH

"I was delivered out of the mouth of the lion." Who delivered Paul? God. And Paul said, "The Lord shall deliver me from every evil work."

Faith brought results to Paul.

1. His faith saved him, yes, simple faith in the crucified, risen Son of God. The same faith in Christ will save you, my lost friend. Jesus said, "Verily, verily, I say unto you, he that believeth on me hath everlasting life."

2. His faith sent him. God called him, and Paul answered. He moved out by faith. He was sent out on his missionary tours by the Holy Spirit, who said, "Separate me Barnabas and Saul for the work whereunto I have called them."

I talked to a poor man—I say a poor man, but he lives in an expensive home and has a wonderful job making good money. He has a nice family. Listen to what he said to me: "God has called me into full-time service. I am forty-one, so I need to get started right now at the work God wants me to do. But my wife won't go with me. She refuses to leave the home. She will not agree to follow me if I answer God's call and go out in service."

This man testified to his salvation and said, "I know that God has given me a call," but he is still standing still. Not so with the Apostle Paul! His faith sent him.

3. His faith sustained him. In the miserable, lonely hours, Paul's faith sustained him. In the prison cells, his faith kept him strong. When he was beaten with rods, stoned and left for dead, his faith saw him through. In weariness and painfulness, in hunger and thirst, in cold and nakedness, his faith sustained him. FAITH HAS POWER!

Jesus commands, "Have faith in God," such faith in God that you will obey His every command, such faith in God that you will fight sin, such faith in God that you will lift up Christ, such faith in God that you will obey Him!

III. THE FULFILLMENT OF HIS FAITH

"And the Lord shall deliver me from every evil work, and will preserve me unto his heavenly kingdom: to whom be glory for ever and ever. Amen" (II Tim. 4:18). Paul's faith didn't fail. The Lord cannot fail. Our faith and God's faithfulness make an unbeatable combination.

1. Paul's faith has been pictured to let us see the value of strong faith.

> Oh, for a faith that will not shrink
>   Though pressed by every foe,
> That will not tremble on the brink
>   Of any earthly woe;
>
> That will not murmur nor complain
>   Beneath the chastening rod,
> But in the hour of grief or pain
>   Will lean upon its God;
>
> A faith that shines more bright and clear
>   When tempests rage without,
> That when in danger knows no fear,
>   In darkness feels no doubt.
>
> Lord, give us such a faith as this,
>   And then, whate'er may come,
> We'll taste e'en here the hallowed bliss
>   Of an eternal home.

The French sculptor Rodin was accustomed to carrying about a tiny but exquisite piece of sculpture. He would frequently take it from his pocket to study intently its beauty. He declared that he found encouragement for his work by constantly keeping before him this example of the best work which was produced in an earlier age.

I confess to you that I like to keep before me a picture of Paul and his faithfulness to strengthen my heart and send me on.

In Paul we see the value of a strong faith.

2. His faith brought him into the presence of God. There came the time of his Homegoing: it was then that he was "absent from the body" and "present with the Lord."

Nero had everything of the world, but Nero did not have everything from God. The porticoes of Nero's palace were a mile long. The walls were so arranged as to shower lovely perfumes upon his guests. Nero's crown was worth $500,000. His mules were shod with silver. Nero fished with hooks of gold.

When Nero traveled, a thousand carriages accompanied him to carry his wardrobe. It is said of Nero that he never wore a garment the second time.

Nero had nothing—he knew not the Saviour! He had no faith in God. His arm had conquered, but his heart was dissatisfied.

Oh, but Paul had faith in Jesus Christ! He had peace. He had salvation. He had the hope of Heaven.

Let me admonish you to do three things:

(1) Fasten your faith in Him. Don't look to man but to God. Don't trust in the circumstances of life but in Christ. Have faith in a Person, not in a principle.

(2) Build your faith by the Word of God. "Faith cometh by hearing, and hearing by the word of God." Therefore, read the Bible. Listen to the Bible. Saturate your life with the Holy Word.

(3) Use your faith to help others. Paul did, and you and I must do likewise.

Dr. James Stewart tells the remarkable story of some twenty Christians in a foreign land who gathered again and again for Bible study. Some people had suggested that they close the doors of the little church and give up, but a few of them held on. They kept on praying. They kept on studying the Bible. Their faith was mighty. They were poor, but they brought their tithes into the church and laid them upon the altar. They kept on seeking the face of God.

The largest thing in their lives was their faith. It was the one thing that crowded their horizons. It was the theme of their talk at all times.

Then Dr. Stewart said that he went to hold a meeting in that strange and spiritually desolate place. In the course of the meetings, hundreds of souls were saved. The building seated some 800 people, and it was packed for every service.

The people didn't have a pastor, but they established twenty mission stations in the area around them. They went on to work mightily, though they had nothing from a human standpoint.

Use your faith! Go on and accomplish the work God has for you to do!

I remind you that faith doesn't hide the difficulties nor belittle them. If you would have faith, you must look beyond all difficulties and dark places. Satan will war against you. Problems that seem like giants will come against you. In it all, HAVE FAITH IN GOD!

9

The Saddest
Word of Tongue
or Pen

"And I saw a great white throne, and him that sat on it, from whose face the earth and the heaven fled away; and there was found no place for them.

"And I saw the dead, small and great, stand before God; and the books were opened: and another book was opened, which is the book of life: and the dead were judged out of those things which were written in the books, according to their works.

"And the sea gave up the dead which were in it; and death and hell delivered up the dead which were in them: and they were judged every man according to their works.

"And death and hell were cast into the lake of fire. This is the second death.

"And whosoever was not found written in the book of life was cast into the lake of fire."—Rev. 20:11–15.

There are 66 books; 1,189 chapters; 31,173 verses; 773,746 words; and 3,566,490 letters in the Bible.

In the Old Testament there are 39 books; 929 chapters; 23,214 verses; 592,493 words; and 2,728,110 letters.

In the New Testament there are 27 books; 260 chapters;

7,959 verses; 181,253 words; 838,380 letters.

I repeat, there are 773,746 words in the Bible, but one word is the saddest of all.

An unabridged dictionary of 1961 has a total of 6,165,000 words. Big words, little words, hard words, easy words—but one word out of all the immensity of over 6,000,000 stands out as the saddest of all.

As I began thinking about words in the Bible, I thought of happy words. David the singer was continually rejoicing in the Lord. He said, "O give thanks unto the Lord, for he is good: for his mercy endureth for ever." Again, we find the psalmist crying, "O praise the Lord, all ye nations: praise him, all ye people." Come to the book of Philippians, and we find the note of praise again. Paul said, "Rejoice in the Lord alway: and again I say, Rejoice."

I thought also of healing words as coming to us from the Bible. The loving Saviour often spoke words of healing to the sick, the blind and the paralytic coming to Him. He forgave the sins of the palsied man of Mark 2 and then commanded him to take up his bed and walk.

I think also of commanding words:

"Go ye therefore, and teach all nations, baptizing them in the name of the Father, and of the Son, and of the Holy Ghost:

"Teaching them to observe all things whatsoever I have commanded you: and, lo, I am with you alway, even unto the end of the world."—Matt. 28:19, 20.

When we think about words in the Bible, we are forced to think about critical words. The Pharisees often came against the Lord and criticized His life and teachings. If He healed a man on the Sabbath day, they criticized.

I thought also of sad words appearing in the Bible; especially my heart went to the words in Matthew 23:37-39 when Jesus said,

"O Jerusalem, Jerusalem, thou that killest the prophets, and stonest them which are sent unto thee, how often would I have gathered thy children together, even as a hen gathereth her chickens under her wings, and ye would not!

"Behold, your house is left unto you desolate.

"For I say unto you, Ye shall not see me henceforth, till ye shall say, Blessed is he that cometh in the name of the Lord."

But, my friends, I believe the saddest word in the Bible occurs in Luke 19:10, "For the Son of man is come to seek and to save that which was *lost.*"

This Bible tells us that men without Christ are lost. Men who die without Christ are forever separated from Him and from Heaven. Without Him men are lost throughout all eternity. We read, "He that believeth on him is not condemned: but he that believeth not is condemned already, because he hath not believed in the name of the only begotten Son of God" (John 3:18). We read, "He that believeth on the Son hath everlasting life: and he that believeth not the Son shall not see life; but the wrath of God abideth on him" (John 3:36).

There is coming a judgment of the lost (Rev. 20:11–15). Of all the judgments, this is the hardest. But the Bible speaks of five judgments.

1. The judgment of the believer's sins on the cross of Christ. When we accept Jesus as Saviour, our eternal destiny is settled forever. We have passed from death unto life.

2. The judgment of self. "For if we would judge ourselves, we should not be judged."

3. The judgment seat of Christ portrayed in the Word of God. Read Romans 14:10–12 and I Corinthians 3:11–15.

4. The judgment of living nations as given to us in Matthew 25. This judgment takes place at the revelation of Christ when He shall sit upon the throne of His glory.

5. The great white throne judgment. This is the final scene before we come to read about the new Heaven and the new earth.

The great white throne judgment is the judgment of the lost when the dead, small and great, stand before God and the books are opened. It requires books to register the wicked. A single book suffices for inclusion of the righteous.

The wicked are judged according to their works (Rev. 20:13). The wicked of all the ages will stand in this judgment. Death and Hell give up the dead which are in them, and they are judged. They are committed to the second death. The second death is the lake of fire.

The great white throne judgment is the judgment of the *lost*. Think of that word for a few moments.

I. LOST—A WORD OF HOPELESSNESS

While I was visiting in a penitentiary, the chaplain took me near Death Row. He said, "We have one man awaiting death. Nothing more can be done for him. He will go to the chair in a few hours. His case is hopeless."

The man without Christ stands at the great white throne judgment—lost forever!

The finality of this judgment is pictured in Luke 16 in the story given by the Lord Jesus: "The beggar died, and was carried by the angels into Abraham's bosom: the rich man also died, and was buried; And in Hell he lift up his eyes, being in torments" (vss. 22, 23).

The rich man made a plea, but the plea came too late. "Father Abraham, have mercy on me, and send Lazarus, that he may dip the tip of his finger in water, and cool my tongue; for I am tormented in this flame."

Here is the story of a man who had everything on earth—everything that money could buy—but in Hell he is begging for a single drop of water!

One day he was rich; the next day, a beggar. The reverse was true of Lazarus. One day he was a beggar; the next day he was enjoying the riches of God.

Perhaps one day the rich man told about the beggar at his gate. His drinking companions laughed about the poor, sore-covered beggar who lay at the gate. But when death came, the rich man left his palace, his gardens, his friends; and in Hell "he lift up his eyes, being in torments." He was lost forever!

II. LOST—A WORD OF SUFFERING

Again, we turn to the story in Luke 16. Notice how it illustrates this point of my message.

1. The rich man had the suffering of desire never granted. He wanted water but never got it. Doubtless he had never appreciated water when he was upon the earth. No doubt he had rivers of clear water cutting across his vast estate and fountains of water which threw their sprays all over his landscape. This abundance of water meant nothing to Dives, but in Hell he is crying for a drop of water.

2. *The rich man had the suffering of a working memory.* Memory will be retained in Hell. Abraham said to Dives, "Son, remember that thou in thy lifetime receivedst thy good things, and likewise Lazarus evil things: but now he is comforted, and thou art tormented."

Memory will be a part of Hell. All of the modernists, the fiction writers, the sophisticates cannot change this fact. The rich man in Hell had eternity to remember his failure.

Someone recounts this story from the Civil War:

> A chaplain came to a man who had a serious injury and was slowly bleeding to death. The chaplain gave assistance and, while he was doing so, talked to the man about repentance and faith in Christ. The soldier told the chaplain that he had lived without God and he would die without God.
>
> But as the chaplain dealt with him, he went into a trance. He dreamed that he was walking the corridors of Hell. He felt searing drops of water falling down on his lost soul. He said to an attendant of Satan, "What is that which is falling with such searing heat upon my soul?" To which the inhabitant of Hell answered, "Those are the tears of your mother."
>
> When the soldier opened his eyes again, he said to the chaplain, "I just dreamed that I was in Hell. My mother's tears were there. I remembered her every prayer for me, every tear she shed for me. And if memory is in Hell, Chaplain, I don't want to go there. Start telling me again how to be saved; this time I will listen and obey."

3. *The suffering of Hell is revealed in these words of Abraham,* "between us and you there is a great gulf fixed." Hell is a place of suffering—suffering for eternity. The rich man cried for help but received none.

Some time ago I saw a man in chains in the Erlanger Hospital. He couldn't leave the bed, but I could walk up to his bed and talk to him. Though in chains, he still had the comfort of friends and loved ones. But in Hell, "there is a great gulf fixed."

III. LOST—A WORD OF SHAME

What makes a man a lost man? The Bible tells us very plainly. Jesus said, "He that believeth not is condemned already." Being lost is not a matter of many sins; it is the matter of one sin—the sin of unbelief, the sin of rejection.

The great white throne judgment will intensify:

the shame of rejecting the Lord Jesus Christ;

the shame of rejecting One who never harmed a soul in this world;

the shame of rejecting One who desires to give salvation to everyone;

the shame of rejecting One who went to the cross and shed His blood to make atonement for our sins;

the shame of rejecting One who pleaded with men to receive Him;

the shame of rejecting God's only begotten Son;

the shame of turning your back upon the invitations to be saved, given on every page of the Word of God.

I have met many men who have had to bear the marks of shame throughout a lifetime. One man confessed to me that he had killed a man some years ago. He had served time in a penitentiary, then was released. But somehow he could never get away from the shame of what he had done. Some men confess to the shame of stealing; others confess to the shame of wrecking the home of another person.

There is much to be ashamed of in this shameless, evil world. But the greatest shame of all will be the shame of a man who rejects Jesus Christ. And this shame will extend throughout eternity.

IV. LOST—A WORD OF CHALLENGE

Lost! Men without Christ are eternally lost! How this should stir us to new work!

This church is here to reach the lost. Highland Park Baptist Church sends out missionaries to every field of the world—to reach the lost. We have established forty-eight chapels [more, in later years] in and around the city—to reach the lost. We run eighteen buses [more, in later years] on Sunday morning—to reach the lost. We run a Sunday school and Baptist training union—to reach the lost. We broadcast thirty minutes every day—to reach the lost. We operate Camp Joy throughout the summer—to reach the lost. We have revivals, Bible conferences and missionary conferences—to reach the lost. We operate Tennessee Temple Schools—university, Bible school, seminary, high school and elementary school—to reach the lost. It is our business as a church to use all means to bring people to Christ.

This is the task of the individual Christian—we are here to reach the lost. We have been commissioned, we have been called, we have been set aside.

We are trying to picture for you in this message the judgment of the lost dead, who will be judged out of the books. Everyone's sins will be plainly written down. God will judge each one out of the record. No Christian will stand at the great white throne to decide salvation: that has been settled already. They stand there as lost sinners to find out the amount of their punishment in Hell forever.

All sins will be brought to light, for remember, these are sinners who have not had their sins covered by the blood of Jesus. Sinner, there are many things which you have done which no one but God knows about. He has it all written down in the record, and one day, if you die without Christ, you will face it.

Sins never committed openly will also be brought to light. Jesus said, "But I say unto you, That whosoever looketh on a woman to lust after her hath committed adultery with her already in his heart" (Matt. 5:28). John tells us in I John 3:15, "Whosoever hateth his brother is a murderer: and ye know that no murderer hath eternal life abiding in him."

What is the outcome of this judgment? It is written down for us in Revelation 20, verses 14 and 15, "And death and hell were cast into the lake of fire. This is the second death. And whosoever was not found written in the book of life was cast into the lake of fire."

And still people say, "Well, I know this is true, but there is plenty of time yet." Only recently a man smiled and said that to me. How foolish, how tragic, how devoid of common sense it is to make such a statement!

Doubtless the seven people who were recently killed in a two-car collision thought there was "plenty of time yet." Doubtless of the thirty-five passengers killed on the jet airliner that crashed in the Everglades of Florida, many had said, "Plenty of time yet!" Maybe that is what the four pilots said in Atlanta, Georgia, who were killed in the crash of a beautiful new jet.

I was coming into Atlanta on another airline and looked down toward the field. In the distance I could see a beautiful new jet going down the runway. It went into position, then took off, went into the air five hundred feet, then a thousand feet; and suddenly there was a flash of flame and smoke. The jet airliner had exploded.

The plane on which I was riding could not land. We flew to Macon, Georgia, stayed there for a few minutes, then flew back to Atlanta. When I walked into the airport and asked the young man at the desk what had happened, with tears in his eyes he said, "I have lost the four best friends I had in the world. The four pilots were testing the new jet, and they were my friends. They are gone."

Perhaps those four men had said, "Plenty of time yet!" But there was no time. They went out to meet God in a second. No time for repentance.

My friend, I call upon you to believe in Jesus Christ at this moment.

10

The Voice
of God

"And the Lord said...."—Exod. 3:7.

More than two thousand times in the Old Testament we read where God spoke. We find words such as these again and again:

"And the Lord said...."

"Then the Lord said unto Moses...."

"And the Lord spake...."

"Hear the word of the Lord...."

"I heard the voice of the Lord say...."

"God spake unto Israel...."

The Bible, from the first word of Genesis to the last word of Revelation, is the voice of God speaking unto us.

I believe what Paul said to young Timothy:

"All scripture is given by inspiration of God, and is profitable for doctrine, for reproof, for correction, for instruction in righteousness:

"That the man of God may be perfect, throughly furnished unto all good works."—II Tim. 3:16, 17.

By this Word, God speaks to us. We don't hear His words through present-day magazines or filthy paperbacks. We don't hear His words as we read the newspapers, listen to the radio and watch television. The message of God comes to us by His Word.

A few days ago I visited a man in one of our hospitals. As I stood by his bedside, I noticed the magazines. On the blanket at his side was a package of playing cards. On the table next to the bed was a package or two of cigarettes.

I said, "Sir, are you a Christian?"

"Of course I am. I belong to your church," he replied.

"Where is your Bible?"

"Oh, I didn't bring it with me."

"How long have you been here?"

He stated that he had been in the hospital a number of weeks. No Bible, just magazines, playing cards and cigarettes. I told him that he could have a Gideon Bible by simply asking the nurse to bring him one.

The truth is, the man had no desire for a Bible. Saved? A Christian man? That is not for us to say. But perhaps by that illustration I can lay upon your hearts the great necessity to read the Word of God in order to hear the voice of God.

Christian friend, are you reading your Bible? Do you read it every day? Do you seek some truth for your own heart?

Now let us consider the voice of God.

I. GOD SPEAKS AUTHORITATIVELY

This is God's Word! And God's Word is true. "In hope of eternal life, which God, that cannot lie, promised before the world began" (Titus 1:2).

This Word is indestructible! "Heaven and earth shall pass away, but my words shall not pass away" (Matt. 24:35).

Someone put it down in this fashion:

Century follows century—there It stands.
Empires rise and fall and are forgotten—there It stands.
Dynasty succeeds dynasty—there It stands.
Kings are crowned and uncrowned—there It stands.
Emperors decree Its extermination—there It stands.
Atheists rail against It—there It stands.

Agnostics smile cynically—there It stands.
Profane, prayerless punsters caricature It—there It stands.
Unbelief abandons It—there It stands.
Higher critics deny Its claim to any inspiration—there It stands.
The flames are kindled about It—there It stands.
The tooth of time gnaws but makes no dent in It—there It stands.
Infidels predict Its abandonment—there It stands.
Modernism tries to explain It away—there It stands.

Let me suggest three things that you should do regarding this authoritative Word of God.

1. *Respect the Word.* Never allow yourself to make light of this holy, infallible Word of God. Occasionally I meet some lighthearted smart aleck who laughs at some of God's teaching. Respect the Bible!

2. *Read the Word.* "He that hath ears to hear, let him hear."

A few days ago I spoke about the Bible and quoted Dr. Howard M. Kelly. I would like to give another statement by this medical doctor:

> The great effective instrument of the Holy Spirit by which the truth is authoritatively taught is the inspired Word of God. Satan is gaining victories by holding men back from a loving, searching study of the Bible.
>
> My own daily life is as full as that of any man I know; but I have found long since that, as I allow the pressure of professional and other engagements to fill in every moment between rising and going to bed, the spirit would surely starve. So I made a rule which I have since stuck to, in spite of many temptations, and that is, not to read or study anything except my Bible after the evening meal and never to read any other book but the Bible on Sunday.

A friend was calling upon a young mother. She found her sitting in a chair holding her baby, and in her hand was a Bible. The friend said humorously, "Are you reading to your baby?"

"Yes," the young mother replied.

"But do you think he understands?"

"He doesn't understand now, but I want his earliest memories to be that of hearing God's Word."

The mother had it right. God's Word is the Sword of the Spirit. It is this Word that we need to hear from the cradle to the grave. Read your Bible. Study it. Heed its teachings.

3. Yes, *obey the Word.* Jesus said, "Ye are my friends, if ye do whatsoever I command you."

The sorry, stumbling lives of people today are the result of not obeying the Word of God.

Michael Faraday's faith in the Bible is well known. One day when he was ill, his friend found him resting his head on a table on which lay an open Book.

"I fear you are worse today," his friend said.

"No," answered Faraday. "It is not that. But why," he asked with his hand upon the Bible, "will people go astray when they have this blessed Book to guide them?"

I repeat: this is God's Word. Hear it. Heed it. Follow it!

II. GOD SPEAKS UNDERSTANDINGLY

The Lord spoke to Moses in a most unusual and amazing way— out of a burning bush. He said, "Moses, Moses." Moses answered, "Here am I."

God commanded Moses to go down and deliver the people of Israel out of Egyptian bondage. But Moses said, "Who am I, that I should go unto Pharaoh, and that I should bring forth the children of Israel out of Egypt?" The Lord said, 'I will be with you, and I will guide you.'

But Moses asked for still more: "Behold, when I come unto the children of Israel, and shall say unto them, The God of your fathers hath sent me unto you; and they shall say to me, What is his name? what shall I say unto them?" God said to Moses, "I AM THAT I AM. . . . Thus shalt thou say unto the children of Israel, I AM hath sent me unto you."

In the Bible God called Himself by various names. One name is *Jehovah-Jireh* which means "the Lord will provide." Another, *Jehovah-Nissi,* means "the Lord my banner." Many other titles are given to our Lord; but "I AM" encompassed them all. In taking this title, Jehovah was furnishing His people with a blank check to be filled in for any amount.

Jesus said, "I am the way, the truth, and the life." How blessed to receive the great "I AM"!

We recall that God spoke understandingly to Moses. Moses gave some objections and said that he could not speak. He first said that the people would not believe him. Then he said, "I am not eloquent." The Lord gave him Aaron as the spokesman.

God knows all about you. He knows your strength and your weakness. Strangely, the Lord will choose that which is weak to accomplish His great purposes. God takes up the weakest instruments to accomplish His mightiest ends. We read about "a rod," "a ram's horn," "a cake of barley meal," "an earthen pitcher," "a shepherd's sling"—anything to accomplish His work.

Men imagine that splendid ends can only be reached by splendid means, but such is not God's way. He can use a crawling worm as well as the scorching sun. This we find in the story of Jonah.

The Lord God understands your needs. Therefore, follow Him. Don't rebel. He can make a success out of failure. Moses—stumbling, stammering, hesitating—became one of the mightiest men this world has ever known. Simon Peter denied the Lord and swore but became the eloquent preacher of Pentecost and the great Christian leader and evangelist of the first century.

Now God said to Moses, 'I have seen My people. I know their afflictions, their sorrows. I will come down to deliver them out of the hand of the Egyptians'—a plain, simple statement. He had come down to display Himself in sovereign grace to do the whole work of salvation, to accomplish His promise made to Abraham and repeated to Isaac and Jacob. He knew about His people, about their tears and sorrows and bondage; now the understanding God is coming to deliver them.

He was not attracted by their excellencies nor their virtues. It was not on the grounds of any great good which they had accomplished. He knew what was in them, but He came to deliver them in love, in understanding.

III. GOD SPEAKS CORRECTIVELY

Most of us have discovered that to open the Bible and hear God's voice is to be corrected of some weakness, some misdemeanor, some sin.

He understands—we have already spoken of this; now the God of love corrects us. The Father's work is to correct His children. So if you are God's child, you will be corrected. "For whom the Lord loveth he chasteneth, and scourgeth every son whom he receiveth" (Heb. 12:6).

He speaks again and again to His children through the Word, through preachers, through Christian friends, through circumstances, through tragedies.

He spoke to King Saul, King David, Simon Peter, John Mark, and multitudes of others in Bible days; and He speaks to us today.

Listen to His voice. Listen when He speaks to correct you. Perhaps you have a weakness, some sin, some wrong that needs correcting. Perhaps He is using my message, my voice, my reading of the Word of God to speak to your heart. Hear it and obey it, for in love He corrects.

A young child said to her grandmother, "Why do you keep reading your Bible all day, Granny?" Grandmother answered, "Honey, you might say I was cramming for my final examination."

He speaks correctively. He knocks out our self-sufficiency. He punctures our pride. He takes away our selfish plans.

I repeat: the Bible does and should correct.

A heathen Chinese gave a gift Bible back to the missionary, explaining, "Every time I read it, it kicks me."

Moody Monthly gave this story:

A minister sent a number of books, among them a copy of the New Testament, to be rebound. He was surprised on the return of the books to find on the backbone of the New Testament a label in gilt letters, TNT. There was not room to spell out "the New Testament." The Bible is TNT.

The Bible is dynamite. The Bible corrects us.

IV. GOD SPEAKS COMPASSIONATELY

"Have I been so long time with you, and yet hast thou not known me, Philip? he that hath seen me hath seen the Father; and how sayest thou then, Shew us the Father?"—John 14:9.

"But when he saw the multitudes, he was moved with compassion on them, because they fainted, and were scattered abroad, as sheep having no shepherd."—Matt. 9:36.

"And Jesus, moved with compassion, put forth his hand, and touched him, and saith unto him, I will; be thou clean."—Mark 1:41.

"And Jesus, when he came out, saw much people, and was moved with compassion toward them, because they were as sheep not having a shepherd: and he began to teach them many things."—Mark 6:34.

Yes, Christ revealed God to us. Christ showed us the love and compassion of God.

I have a haunting remembrance of a lonely street. It is a street of big buildings, old buildings, dirty buildings. It is a street crowded with cars and people, yet a lonely street. I am referring to Madison Street in Chicago near the Pacific Garden Mission. When I drove down it, I saw scores of men staggering along. It was a bitter cold day. The snow was falling. Poor drunks were staggering into saloons. Some were clinging to telephone poles. Some were hanging onto one another as they staggered down the street.

First, it was sickening to see men in such numbers throwing away God-given lives. It is impossible to describe the filth, the dirt, the poverty of the men I saw. I saw them with rags wrapped around their feet. Though the day was cold, there were but few who had overcoats. All of them had empty, wretched faces as they staggered along.

But I said to myself, *How does God see them?* I began to wonder, *Does He love them? Is He concerned about those poor drunks, staggering miserably down the street trying to reach the next saloon?*

As we drove on, a few blocks away we saw beautiful and big apartment houses. The first eight or ten floors were garages for the expensive cars of the occupants. Then towering many stories into the sky were the Marina Apartments. They were so arranged that the people could come out of their apartments, go down an elevator, get into their expensive boats, and go out onto Lake Michigan. Or they could come from their rooms, get into a car and drive to work. Someone said that many of the apartments rented for thousands of dollars a month.

Then the truth hit me: *God looks at all in the same way.* He has compassion for the poor drunk on Madison Avenue and for the hardened sinner living in the swanky apartment. Each one without Christ is lost in sin and bound for Hell. Each must come and take of the Lord's compassion. To be saved, each must come before the same cross, look up to the same Saviour, and receive the same Lord Jesus.

Hear, my friend, the voice of God. He invites you to come with every burden, with every heartache, with every need.

"Come unto me, all ye that labour and are heavy laden, and I will give you rest."—Matt. 11:28.

"Ho, every one that thirsteth, come ye to the waters, and he that hath no money; come ye, buy, and eat; yea, come, buy wine and milk without money and without price."—Isa. 55:1.

The invitation is to you. Will you come to the Saviour? He is ready to save you now. Oh, listen to His voice as He calls lovingly, pleadingly, compassionately!

11

The World Standing Before God

"For therein is the righteousness of God revealed from faith to faith: as it is written, The just shall live by faith.

"For the wrath of God is revealed from heaven against all ungodliness and unrighteousness of men, who hold the truth in unrighteousness."—Rom. 1:17, 18.

Salvation is the theme of the book of Romans. The first eight chapters and the last five speak of the salvation which God has for all. Chapters nine through eleven speak of Israel and God's dealing with the people. The first eight chapters are doctrinal. Chapters nine through eleven are dispensational. Chapters twelve through sixteen deal with salvation and the practical life of the individual.

Throughout the book of Romans, I get a picture of the world standing before God—Jew and Gentile. The world stands before a God of love. Paul said, "But God commendeth his love toward us, in that, while we were yet sinners, Christ died for us."

The world stands before a God of judgment. Sin always brings judgment. "For the wages of sin is death...." God cannot look upon sin with any degree of toleration. Sin must be judged—all sin.

The world stands before a God of long-suffering. Peter said, "The

Lord is not slack concerning his promise, as some men count slackness; but is longsuffering to us-ward, not willing that any should perish, but that all should come to repentance" (II Pet. 3:9).

The world stands before a God of unlimited generosity. The Lord giveth to all men liberally. Blessings are poured out upon saints and sinners. Abundant blessings come upon the children of God who come before Him with all their needs. He gives us salvation, peace of heart and abundant living.

Now we shall think primarily upon Romans 1, 2 and 3 as we consider "The World Standing Before God."

I. THE BRILLIANCE OF A MAN'S TESTIMONY

"Paul, a servant of Jesus Christ, called to be an apostle, separated unto the gospel of God."—Rom. 1:1.

"For I am not ashamed of the gospel of Christ: for it is the power of God unto salvation to every one that believeth; to the Jew first, and also to the Greek."—Rom. 1:16.

As we begin this book of Romans, we are faced with the brilliant testimony of one who knew the Lord.

1. *Paul's great salvation.* Remember, Paul hated Christians; and as a Pharisee, he went everywhere seeking to bring them to prison and to destroy them if possible.

In Acts 9:1 and 2, we read:

"And Saul, yet breathing out threatenings and slaughter against the disciples of the Lord, went unto the high priest, And desired of him letters to Damascus to the synagogues, that if he found any of this way, whether they were men or women, he might bring them bound unto Jerusalem."

Following that introduction, we find the glorious story of Paul seeing a light from Heaven and hearing the voice of the Lord Jesus. This brought him to the end of himself and to the Saviour.

Saul of Tarsus was saved from bitterness—the bitterness of those who know not Christ.

Saul was saved from eternal Hell—separation from God.

Saul was saved from eternal torment—the everlasting agony of those who go down into the pit of Hell.

Rejoice about your salvation! Make much of it! Tell people when you were saved and something of the circumstances surrounding your salvation.

Pat Withrow spoke in this church a number of times. He founded the Union Mission in Charleston, West Virginia, and for some forty-five years did a monumental work in that city, reaching the poor, the outcasts, the drunkards, the dope fiends, the forgotten men and women. You recall that Pat Withrow preached here at one time for a week. He stood in the pulpit, dressed in a nice suit and wearing a disreputable pair of houseshoes. When I questioned him about why he wore the houseshoes, he made a very simple answer: "They feel better than shoes."

Pat Withrow knew how to lead people to the Saviour. And he knew more than that. He knew how to help a man stick to his faith and to grow in grace. When I would make my trips to Charleston for meetings, he would meet me at the airport.

As we came to his car in the parking lot, a certain man would be standing at the rear door. He would open it and we would get in. Then he would get in the front seat and start driving.

As soon as we left the parking place, Pat Withrow would turn to him and say, "Jim (George, John, whatever his name was), tell Brother Roberson what the Lord has done for you."

Immediately he would begin speaking: "I was saved one month, six days, and six hours ago. I know that Christ is my Saviour, and I am rejoicing that He has redeemed me."

I listened to this so many times that I had to ask Mr. Withrow why he had the man do this. Pat said, "I have discovered that, if you want a man to grow in grace and be steady in the things of God, you keep him close to his salvation experience."

Paul never got away from that experience on the Damascus road, and he told about his salvation experience there many a time.

2. *Paul's great debt.* "I am a debtor both to the Greeks, and to the Barbarians; both to the wise, and to the unwise. So, as much as

in me is, I am ready to preach the gospel to you that are at Rome also" (Rom. 1:14, 15). Because of his salvation, Paul felt that he owed a debt to the Lord. He was saved; now in response to his salvation, he must tell the message to all people.

3. *Paul's great faith.* He had no doubt about the power of the Gospel and what it could do. He believed that the Gospel is "the power of God unto salvation to every one that believeth; to the Jew first, and also to the Greek."

In this wicked, shadowy, modernistic day, many doubt the power of the Gospel. Even church leaders are prone to try about everything before they will come to the Gospel of Jesus Christ.

Can you not see the brightness, the brilliance of this man's testimony? He knew what he was. He knew what God had done for him. And he rejoiced in it.

II. THE BLACKNESS OF MAN'S SIN

A picture of sin is given to us in the book of Romans.

"And even as they did not like to retain God in their knowledge, God gave them over to a reprobate mind, to do those things which are not convenient;

"Being filled with all unrighteousness, fornication, wickedness, covetousness, maliciousness; full of envy, murder, debate, deceit, malignity; whisperers,

"Backbiters, haters of God, despiteful, proud, boasters, inventors of evil things, disobedient to parents,

"Without understanding, covenant breakers, without natural affection, implacable, unmerciful:

"Who knowing the judgment of God, that they which commit such things are worthy of death, not only do the same, but have pleasure in them that do them." —Rom. 1:28–32.

". . . in the day when God shall judge the secrets of men by Jesus Christ according to my gospel.

"Behold, thou art called a Jew, and restest in the law, and makest thy boast of God,

"And knowest his will, and approvest the things that are more

excellent, being instructed out of the law;

"And art confident that thou thyself art a guide of the blind, a light of them which are in darkness,

"An instructor of the foolish, a teacher of babes, which hast the form of knowledge and of the truth in the law. ˙

"Thou therefore which teachest another, teachest thou not thyself? thou that preachest a man should not steal, dost thou steal?

"Thou that sayest a man should not commit adultery, dost thou commit adultery? thou that abhorrest idols, dost thou commit sacrilege?

"Thou that makest thy boast of the law, through breaking the law dishonourest thou God?

"For the name of God is blasphemed among the Gentiles through you, as it is written.

"For circumcision verily profiteth, if thou keep the law: but if thou be a breaker of the law, thy circumcision is made uncircumcision."— Rom. 2:16–25.

"What then? are we better than they? No, in no wise: for we have before proved both Jews and Gentiles, that they are all under sin;

"As it is written, There is none righteous, no, not one:

"There is none that understandeth, there is none that seeketh after God.

"They are all gone out of the way, they are together become unprofitable; there is none that doeth good, no, not one.

"Their throat is an open sepulchre; with their tongues they have used deceit; the poison of asps is under their lips:

"Whose mouth is full of cursing and bitterness:

"Their feet are swift to shed blood:

"Destruction and misery are in their ways:

"And the way of peace have they not known:

"There is no fear of God before their eyes."—Rom. 3:9–18.

All men are sinners—both Jews and Gentiles. In Romans 3:23 we read, "For all have sinned, and come short of the glory of God." The whole world is guilty before the Lord.

I was conducting services in a distant city. In the course of my meeting, I had people give a few testimonies.

One lady arose to say that she was witnessing to the Jews. I was pleased to hear this and stated so. Then I said, "Jews without Christ are lost and Hell-bound." Strangely, she seemed to resent it. She shook her head negatively. I sensed at once that she was trying to give some special touch to Jewish people.

In this she was wrong. This Bible says, "All have sinned, and come short of the glory of God." That means Jews and Gentiles alike.

1. *The definition of sin.* "Sin is the transgression of the law." That definition is a little tame for this day. Man must see the awfulness of sin as expressed in the words of Paul.

2. *The direction of sin.* Sin always leads away from God. Sin always brings men downward.

A pastor had in his congregation a very cultured woman. She was talented and educated. He knew that she would be a good Sunday schoolteacher and a fine leader for young people if she would only consecrate her life to the Lord.

On a number of occasions, he talked to her about it. She told him, "Oh, I would dearly love to do that, but I have so many responsibilities. I belong to this, and I belong to that. And all make such heavy demands upon me. I just haven't the time for anything else."

In the home of this lady lived a nephew, a charming young man when he was sober. Drink was dragging him down. After a binge he would seclude himself sometimes for days, ashamed to meet his friends.

One day a deacon in the church called the pastor and said, "Young Mr. So-and-so committed suicide this morning, and his aunt is calling for you. Please come over at once."

The pastor hurried to the home where the young man lay a corpse. He was shown into the room where the stricken woman lay quietly on the bed. Her head was covered by a handkerchief. As he approached he said quietly, "Mrs. _____, I have come."

She threw up her arms and let out a wail—a cry of agony. "Oh, I let him slip through my fingers into Hell!"

Yes, she was so busy with her clubs and social affairs that she let her charming nephew go down into Hell. Sin always leads downward.

3. *The destiny of the sinner.* "He that believeth not is condemned already." The destiny of the sinner is Hell. The sinner is eternally lost without Jesus Christ. Sin brings judgment, and judgment brings Hell.

Oh, the blackness of sin! the awfulness of the future of those who despise the riches of God's grace!

I don't think we have had any story that seemed to carry so much pathos as the one given years ago in the newspapers regarding the daughter of Art Linkletter. The paper told the story very simply. She had her own apartment, though only twenty years of age. She had not married. She started taking dope. Her father had talked to her about it, but apparently she had continued taking it. Her death came when she jumped from the window of her apartment. In the apartment was a man twenty-seven years of age.

I gave you something of that terrible story just to emphasize this word *blackness.* Sin is black. Sin is hellish.

III. THE BURDEN OF GOD'S HEART

Words are so inadequate. God looks upon the world. He sees a lost man and desires man's salvation. The love of God is pictured throughout the Word of God.

The burden of God's heart—I build this on two things: first, upon the scriptural account of Christ Himself. The Son of God who came to reveal God to us shows us God's burdened heart.

Jesus said, "He that hath seen me hath seen the Father." Christ revealed the Father to us. Jesus, as He looked upon the city of Jerusalem, cried,

"O Jerusalem, Jerusalem, thou that killest the prophets, and stonest them which are sent unto thee, how often would I have gathered thy children together, even as a hen gathereth her chickens under her wings, and ye would not!"—Matt. 23:37.

In Luke 19:41 we read, "And when he was come near, he beheld the city, and wept over it." When we see the concern of our Saviour for people, we remind ourselves that this is the concern of our eternal Heavenly Father.

Second, the burden of God's heart is revealed in the book of Romans. Paul was used of God to write this book, but it is God's book! His heart of love and longing is shown to us here:

"Who is he that condemneth? It is Christ that died, yea rather, that is risen again, who is even at the right hand of God, who also maketh intercession for us.

"Who shall separate us from the love of Christ? shall tribulation, or distress, or persecution, or famine, or nakedness, or peril, or sword?"—Rom. 8:34, 35.

Paul expresses the great concern of our God in these words:

"I say the truth in Christ, I lie not, my conscience also bearing me witness in the Holy Ghost,

"That I have great heaviness and continual sorrow in my heart.

"For I could wish that myself were accursed from Christ for my brethren, my kinsmen according to the flesh."—Rom. 9:1–3.

The love of God is beautifully expressed to us in these words:

"But what saith it? The word is nigh thee, even in thy mouth, and in thy heart: that is, the word of faith, which we preach;

"That if thou shalt confess with thy mouth the Lord Jesus, and shalt believe in thine heart that God hath raised him from the dead, thou shalt be saved.

"For with the heart man believeth unto righteousness; and with the mouth confession is made unto salvation."—Rom. 10:8–10.

We see God's love despite man's wicked actions. "God so loved the world, that he gave his only begotten Son." We see the rebellion of man against every overture of God's grace. Prophets were sent, apostles were sent, but man rebelled. Still God loved on!

We have often mentioned the name of Sam Hadley of Water Street Mission, New York City. Mr. Hadley told the story of a man who hit bottom. He had ranked high in the legal profession until he became a hopeless drunkard. To avoid embarrassing his family, he ran away to the big city. When hungry, he went to the mission for something to eat.

Mr. Hadley took him to his home, put new clothes on him and fed him. After three months, the man vanished. Eventually Mr. Hadley heard that he had been sent to prison for a year for theft, then let out. After a prolonged drunk, he was back at the mission for food and clothes.

Mr. Hadley again invited him to be a guest in his home. After a few weeks of witnessing to him, the man told him that he had no intention of being a Christian. He scoffed at Mr. Hadley and said he only came to him to get food and clothes. Then he told Mr. Hadley that he would never come back again.

Some months later Mr. Hadley revealed how he saw in one of the city papers that this man had been run down on the street by a reckless driver and was near death in the charity ward of the hospital. The great mission man hurried to the hospital and, kneeling by the cot, said, "Old fellow, I found you. Sorry you are in this fix. Now what can I do for you?"

The bum said, "How can you do this when I treated you so poorly?"

Mr. Hadley told him that he loved him because Jesus loved him; told him of the mighty love of God and of Christ; told him that he was merely there to express God's love to him.

Mr. Hadley then said, "You should have seen him roll over into the arms of Jesus!

"He lived only a few days. His body was brought to the Water Street Mission and given a fine Christian funeral. As I stood looking at this dead face and thought of the battle I had fought for his soul, I took from my coat lapel a beautiful white rose my wife had pinned there that morning, laid it down by his cold face and shouted: 'There, Mr. Devil! Who won the victory in this case—you or me?' "

Again, God loves sinners despite man's wickedness. In Romans 1:30 are the words, "haters of God." There are many people who hate God. Some may express it and some may not, but God knows all about it. Yet He loves on, despite the fact of man's hatred.

A lot of things would quickly change if we could read the minds of others. A lot of friendships would break off speedily if we knew what some people were thinking. But with God, He loves in spite of the hatred embedded in man's wicked heart.

Someone trying to express the love of God told this imaginary story:

A young man, much loved of his mother, pursued a wicked course that took him deeper and deeper into sin. He became enamored of an evil woman who dragged him down further and further. The mother naturally tried her best to draw him back to a higher plane. The other woman resented it bitterly.

One night, the story goes, the evil woman chided the man with an accusation that he didn't really love her. He vowed that he did. She appealed to his drunken mind, saying that if he loved her, he would rid them of his mother and her pleadings.

According to the story, the young man rushed from the room to the nearby house of his mother. He dealt her death blows, tearing the heart from her body to carry it back to his lover.

Then comes the climax of the strange, imaginary story. As he rushed on in his insane folly, he stumbled and fell; and from the bleeding heart there came a voice, "My son, are you hurt?"

That is the way God loves us. God has a burdened heart—a burden for all lost souls. He sent His Son to die upon the cross for us. The death of our Saviour is the chief illustration of the love of God.

IV. THE BUOYANCY OF GOD'S PROMISES

God, in His mercy, reaches down to the lowest depths, takes the sinner by the hand and brings him up to stand upon the rock of everlasting life. We have seen this happen many times. It has transpired in this church again and again. We have seen the joy of salvation come into a man's heart. After years of wickedness, he turns to the Saviour, and God gives him the glorious, transforming joy of the Lord.

Salvation is for everyone who will receive it. "For whosoever shall call upon the name of the Lord shall be saved." "Whosoever" is one of the happiest words in our vocabulary. Come, sinner, whatever your condition of life, whatever your age—come, for He will save you.

Again, God has a plan for every saved soul. When Paul met the Lord on the road to Damascus, he asked, "Lord, what wilt thou have me to do?" God has a plan, a perfect plan, a work for every one of His children. Just as the architect prepares an accurate and detailed drawing for each new building erected under his guidance and instruction, so God, our gracious and loving Heavenly Father, has the perfect, detailed and accurate plan for the life of every Christian. We can expect Him to reveal that plan as we submit to His will. The plan of God for you and me is a *personal* plan. Paul asked, "Lord, what wilt thou have me to do?" Just as God revealed His plan to Paul in a personal way, so will He reveal it to us. Just as it is a personal plan, so it is a *perfect* plan. Just as it is personal and perfect, so it is *practical.*

God's plans for lives always work. And part of God's plan for us is to tell the story of His love to lost sinners. The greatest joy anyone can ever have is to point someone to the Saviour.

Princess Eugenia sold her royal jewels. With the money, she built a hospital for tuberculosis sufferers. She would visit the patients to see that they were well cared for.

A poor woman near death took the hand of the princess and kissed it. Her tears fell upon it. Just then the sun shining through the window cast a light on those tears so that they sparkled like diamonds. "O God," said Eugenia, "I gave Thee my jewels that the poor sufferers might have care; now You have given them back to me in this dying woman's grateful tears!"

In Raleigh, North Carolina, was a man named John Pullin whom Christians called "the wisest man in town." His main business was to serve God and win souls; and he said, "I run my bank to pay expenses."

This little man, with kindly eyes and a friendly manner, was faithful in his church. He loved people and helped everyone he could. He helped many young people go to college. The people of the city knew of his love to others. They stood in awe of a man who was so loved and respected by everyone.

For example, they were having a revival in one of the churches in the city. Two girls of the red-light district sent a note inside the church and asked for prayer. They did pray, and John Pullin said, "I would like to take the evangelist and go to that section of town and try to win them to the Saviour."

They did go. They had a service in the street, and many were saved. Six came to the church and made their professions public. Later John Pullin established a rescue home for fallen girls.

Then one day the news came that John Pullin had suddenly died. The legislature in session adjourned in honor of him. The flag was flown at half-mast. A committee was sent to request that his body lie in state in the capitol building. Rich and poor streamed by for a last look at the city's First Citizen and the friend of all men.

The funeral service was held at a little church where he belonged and worked. At the graveside was a mountain of flowers sent by the young people who had been sent to college by John Pullin.

As people stood at the graveside, there came two prisoners with clanging chains bearing a huge floral anchor. They laid it on his grave. The prisoners had had a meeting. They said, "We want to send two of our own men to express our love for John Pullin."

Some of the women from the red-light district were there. Weeping, they, too, laid their flowers on the grave.

Yes, John Pullin was the wisest man in town. He was a soul winner. He knew the lifting power of God's grace. He presented the message of Jesus to all people.

We have discussed in this message, first, the brilliance of a man's testimony; second, the blackness of man's sin; third, the burden of God's heart; fourth, the buoyancy of God's promises.

Will you come to the Saviour? Will you receive the Lord Jesus now?

12

Living Out Your Faith
on the Job

"Return to thine own house, and shew how great things God hath done unto thee. And he went his way, and published throughout the whole city how great things Jesus had done unto him."—Luke 8:39.

When Peter, Andrew, James and John were saved, they were soon called to leave all and follow Christ.

When Saul of Tarsus was saved, he, too, was called of God for full-time service. He left the old life and joined the cause of Christ.

Full-time service is not easy! Many discouragements and defeats await the Christian. Satanic influences work to nullify the ministry of the preacher or missionary.

But for this message, I am not dealing with the full-time Christian worker. I am talking about the Christian who goes on with his work, whatever it may be, and lives out his faith before others. The title tells the story: "Living Out Your Faith on the Job."

Many young people get saved, and they must continue their schooling. When they go back to school after the great experience of the new birth, they must live and walk with others. It is not easy. The world is never friendly to the Christian.

When I got saved, salvation brought joy to my heart, and I expected others to share that joy. But I soon found that some ignored my salvation experience altogether. It seemed unworthy of notice or mention. This I found annoying for awhile.

(Young people, bear in mind that others may not rejoice at your salvation. You may get saved in the Highland Park Baptist Church and return home to find that your family may ignore the experience that you had. Your friends may say nothing about it.)

Some made critical remarks about my stand for Christ. And some were happy when I got saved. This will happen. Some will ridicule, and some will scoff.

Now I want us to deal with living out your faith on the job. There are some plain suggestions that I give to you.

I. IDENTIFY YOURSELF CLEARLY

Make sure that you are fully aware of all that you have in Jesus Christ. Be able to say with the Apostle Paul, "For the which cause I also suffer these things: nevertheless I am not ashamed: for I know whom I have believed, and am persuaded that he is able to keep that which I have committed unto him against that day" (II Tim. 1:12).

But before you can identify yourself with others, you must first be identified in your own mind and heart. If you know that you are a child of God, then let others know that you have been saved and are now a member of God's family.

1. *Confess happily to your new life.* Regardless of what others may say or think, confess your faith. It is important to tell others of your salvation. Listen to these words from Matthew 10:32, 33:

"Whosoever therefore shall confess me before men, him will I confess also before my Father which is in heaven.

"But whosoever shall deny me before men, him will I also deny before my Father which is in heaven."

Tell people in happy tones that Jesus is your Saviour.

2. *Never make light of your conversion.* Others may laugh at your decision to follow Christ, but don't join with them. That which has happened is of primary importance, so bravely declare yourself on the side of Christ.

Do not join with the scoffers. Some young people have gotten converted; then when someone laughed at their faith and said that now, since they were saved, they couldn't do certain things, they made the cowardly statement, "Oh, I can go on doing just what I have always done."

Simon Peter comes to mind. When Jesus was taken from the Garden of Gethsemane, the Bible says, "And Peter followed afar off." A little maid came up and said, "This man was also with him," but Peter denied it, saying, "Woman, I know him not." A little later when another person said, "Thou art also of them," Peter said, "Man, I am not."

About an hour later, when the third person came and said, "Of a truth this fellow also was with him; for he is a Galilean," Peter said, "Man, I know not what thou sayest." In Matthew's Gospel we find even stronger words: "Then began he to curse and to swear, saying, I know not the man."

How shameful was this action of the apostle! How happy we should be that the Bible gives a better record of this man after he came to himself and received forgiveness from God.

I beseech you in the name of the Lord Jesus Christ that you always be happy and proud to be a Christian. Never make light of your conversion. Never allow others to make foolish, derogatory remarks about Christ and His work in the individual heart.

3. *Engage in those things that identify people.* Attending church is good identification. Be faithful to the services of your church Sunday morning, Sunday evening, and Wednesday evening. Get a good Bible and read it. Talk about the Bible. Ask questions of others regarding the Word of God.

Establish good prayer habits. Return thanks at the table. Do those things that would identify you as one who has been born again.

Let your appearance be that of one born again. Stay far away from any dress or customs that might identify you in the slightest with an evil, gainsaying world.

Let your speech identify you! Let your work on the job, in the office, in the plant, on the streets, speak in such a way that people will know you are a child of God. Avoid all words of profanity. Stay away from every evil thing that might cause someone to doubt your position in Christ.

I trust that I have made this first point very clear. We are discussing living out your faith on the job. To do this, identify yourself clearly with Christians and with the work of God.

II. DEDICATE YOURSELF COMPLETELY

"I beseech you therefore, brethren, by the mercies of God, that ye present your bodies a living sacrifice, holy, acceptable unto God, which is your reasonable service.

"And be not conformed to this world: but be ye transformed by the renewing of your mind, that ye may prove what is that good, and acceptable, and perfect, will of God."—Rom. 12:1, 2.

We see that dedication is both positive and negative. On the negative side this means separation—"And be not conformed to this world...."

I was a new Christian in Louisville, Kentucky, when I had to identify myself with the people of God. I had to make up my mind regarding doubtful and questionable things.

One evening I had been invited to a home. The people were active members of the local church. After awhile they pulled out some card tables and set them up in the living room. The lady of the house brought out some cards and said, "This is a game that we can all play." I knew nothing of the game, and it looked harmless enough to me, but I saw her go to the front windows and pull down the shades. When this young high school boy asked her why, she said, "Some passing by will not understand. They will think because we have cards in our hands that we are engaged in a game of gambling. I don't want them to have any wrong impressions."

I didn't know much about living for Christ; but when she said that, I at once replied, "I don't believe I'll play. If there is some question about this and if it might be misunderstood, then I would rather not play."

This might be a rule for all of us to establish: if there is a doubt about a thing, then we had better turn from it. If there is a question mark, it is usually wrong.

Avoid the questionable. Separate yourself from the world.

Some years ago I was conducting a very fine revival campaign in another state. One evening a handsome man came down the aisle and accepted Christ as Saviour. All the people rejoiced in his salvation. I later learned that many had been praying for him for some time.

I greeted the man as I would greet any new convert. I, too, was happy that he was saved.

A couple of nights later, he came forward again and said, "I know that I am saved, but I can't continue in the business that I have had for many years."

(He had a very fine position in a brewery and had spent a lifetime in making beer. When he got saved, he thought he might continue in this work; but after praying about the matter, he knew that he had to change, and he did.)

Now let us turn to the positive side. The Bible says that we are to "present [our] bodies a living sacrifice, holy, acceptable unto God." We are to be "transformed by the renewing of [our] mind[s]." Plainly, we are to walk as Christians. In business life, no matter what others may say or do, identify with those who know Christ and stand on the positive side of every issue.

Today marks the beginning of National Library Week. I am in favor of this, and I am heartily on the side of those who give their time to the establishment and maintenance of good libraries. Our city is going to celebrate this special week, calling it "MOD WEEK." Staff and students may wear throughout the week "mod" clothes: miniskirts, pantsuits, pantdresses, etc. The purpose is to "break the image of the stereotyped librarian—the long-sleeved, high-necked black dress, hair in bun, etc."

May I quote again from the memo given to the complete staff of the library: "This week can serve to recruit some young people to the profession by indicating that librarians are just as 'swinging' as anyone else." Another paragraph says, "If there are some among you who feel inclined to dress the part of the old-fashioned librarian, you may do so. The only things excluded are short shorts and bathing suits—I believe we would not work in that attire, unless on the beach perhaps."

Now it is evident that those who have positions in the libraries of our city will have to make up their minds about what they wear. If Christians are going to live out their faith on the job, they will have to dress decently and take a positive stand on correct attire.

To everyone who is in the business field, it is your obligation to dedicate yourself completely and positively to the Christian standards. In political life, walk as a Christian. In homelife, walk as a Christian. In school life, walk as a Christian. In every place, live as children of God and manifest an interest in those around you.

A tent meeting was in progress. A young man had been attending regularly but had not accepted the Lord Jesus Christ as his Saviour.

The evangelist came to the young man after the service and said, "Your Christian mother wants you to be a Christian, and your father would be pleased because he is saved and an officer in the church."

The lad was silent for awhile. Then he said thoughtfully, "Perhaps you may not believe what I say, but neither my father nor my mother has ever asked me to be a Christian. I never expect to be until they do."

The evangelist said, "What a shame that I should be obliged to waste one minute of my time or one ounce of my strength trying to persuade mothers and fathers to speak to their children about Christ."

Living out Christ on the job means that we manifest the Lord to others in action and in speech.

III. ACTIVATE YOURSELF ENTIRELY

Oh, yes, there is something for you to do! God has work for everyone! Every Christian is to be a witness! Note that I said "every" Christian! No one must give you a job—you already have one! Jesus said, "Ye shall be witnesses unto me."

1. *This calls for a clean life.* Keep out of your life anything that may be doubtful or that might hinder you from speaking to others. You can't win souls if your influence is a question. "But if thy brother be grieved with thy meat, now walkest thou not charitably. Destroy not him with thy meat, for whom Christ died" (Rom. 14:15).

2. *This calls for a life of prayer.* Prayer is the power line.

In New York City some years ago there was a man named Jerry McAuley. He was saved out of a wretched life, became head of a great mission and did a work that is still known to people the world over.

At Jerry McAuley's funeral, a shabby-looking, aged man came to the men who stood at the front of the church, took off his tall, battered hat, and asked if one of them would take the bunch of white flowers he held in his hand and place them on Jerry McAuley's coffin. Then the poor old man said, "And when you drop them with the rest, Jerry will understand. He was my friend. He will know that they come from Old Joe Chappy." (Mrs. McAuley got that little bunch of flowers and preserved them.) Old Joe had heard Jerry McAuley say often, "When I die—and it may not be long—I want to be on my knees praying for a lost world. I would rather some poor soul, one I was the means of leading to the Lord, put one little rose on my grave than to have the wealth of a millionaire." And it was so! When he died, here came one who had been led to Christ by Jerry McAuley with a little bunch of white flowers to be put on his casket.

Spend time praying for others—for your family, your friends, missionaries, and the lost.

3. *This calls for a spoken witness.* The Bible exhorts us to speak out regarding the Lord Jesus Christ.

An evangelist was scheduled to give an address in a local high school in the town where he was having a meeting. When he met the principal, he was informed that he could speak, but he must not mention the name of Jesus. The evangelist asked if it would be all right to mention George Washington or Abraham Lincoln. The man said, "Oh, yes, you can talk about them." Then the preacher said, "That's strange. When I came down the hallway, I heard the name of Jesus shouted out from the lips of quite a few young people. If they can use His name in that fashion in the hallways, why can't I speak His name from the platform?"

The principal stated again that he couldn't do so. Then the evangelist said, "If I can't speak the name of Jesus Christ to your young people, I will not speak at all." With that, he walked away and left the principal to explain to his high school assembly.

Oh, yes, my friends, speak out for Jesus Christ.

One evening during a season of revival, a friend was praying after this manner for a certain unconverted neighbor: "O Lord, touch that man with Thy finger." The petition was repeated with great earnestness. Then something inside said to him, *Thou art the finger of God! Hast thou ever spoken a single word to him on the question of salvation? Go thou and touch that man, and thy prayer shall be answered.*

Yes, God is calling us to speak for Him. Jesus said, "As my Father hath sent me, even so send I you."

4. *This calls for concern.* There is no way to keep on going and endeavoring to win souls unless there is a definite concern for others. Our hearts must be broken, and we must have a compassion for the lost.

A young artist painted the picture of a forlorn woman and a child out in a storm. This picture got such a hold on him that he laid down the palette and brush, saying, "I must go to the lost instead of painting them!"

He prepared for the ministry and for some time worked in the city slums. At length he resolved, *I must go to that part of the world where men seem to be most hopelessly lost.* That young artist was none other than Bishop Tucker of Uganda, Africa.

Past midnight last Friday evening while studying on this message, I picked up a book and read a true story that touched my heart, the story of a missionary and his wife Jane and their three small children. They had been serving for two years on one of the small islands in the Bahamas.

They were living on a boat because they couldn't find housing on the island.

It was a hard life for a man, a wife and three children. The weather was warm. There was no refrigeration. But the missionary was faithful because he felt that he was in the place God had given him.

On May 20, 1960, the stove broke down. They couldn't cook. The money was running out. They had been unable to buy any supplies. They wondered what to do next.

At about six o'clock that evening, the missionary decided to move the boat a little farther from shore so as to get away from the insects that were tormenting them. When he turned the ignition key to start the engine, he heard a peculiar sound. He said to his helper, "Something dreadful is about to happen." No sooner had he said this when there came an explosion. He was blown through the roof of the cabin. When he came to, he saw that the top of the boat was blown off and the windows were blasted out.

He ran to the back of the boat where the cargo hatches had been blown away. The interior of the boat was an inferno. He looked down into the flames and saw the three children lying there. He snatched three-year-old Donny, then seven-year-old Donna and began pulling them out of the flames. Then he went back and got five-year-old Kathy. With his wife, he brought them all to the bow of the boat. Their clothing was burned off, and their flesh was blackened. The wife said, "All of us will die."

His helper, Carl Whitehouse, had been blown overboard. Somehow he had gotten to land and came back in a small boat. He put the children into it and headed toward the shore.

On shore there was a long period of waiting. They radioed for a plane from Nassau. The children were burned, his wife was burned, and the missionary himself was severely burned in many places.

Finally the plane came and brought two nurses. But they had to be left behind because there was just room for the pilot and the family.

When they got to Nassau, a jeep carried them to the Rassan Clinic. With all lying in the jeep, a doctor was called. He came. When he saw what had happened, he reached into the jeep and picked up Donna. The doctor, dressed in a beautiful white suit, pressed the body of the little girl against him and ran to the hospital. He treated Donna, then Kathy, then Donny, then the parents.

The missionary said, "All that night I talked to God. I called upon Him for help."

Soon after daylight Dr. Rassan said, "Your daughter Donna is dying." The missionary said, "I couldn't believe it. Despite the protest of the nurses, I got out of bed and went into Donna's room. He was right. She was dying." Donna said, "I feel like I am going away, but don't cry. Everything will be all right." The missionary said, "I tried to hold her, but my bandaged arms would not go around her. I laid my head on her little breast. When I looked up and saw that the nurses were weeping, I knew then that she was gone."

After many days father, mother and two children were released from the hospital. There came a plane for their return back to the United States. The loss of their daughter was a great loss, but their hearts were filled with gratitude.

A few days later the missionary was to speak in his father's church in Jamestown, New York. He could not speak, but he stood there and wept. God even used the weeping. The death of the child meant the salvation of many. People heard the story and accepted Jesus as Saviour.

That missionary is back on the field and is continuing with his work of winning souls. From his house he can look down into the harbor and see the shattered bulk of the "Bahama Star" which had blown up. He can walk a few feet and find the grave of his little daughter.

Ah, but he is living out his faith! He is witnessing. He is winning souls. He is doing the task God had given him to do.

13

The Greatest Battle in History

"And the Lord shall utter his voice before his army: for his camp is very great: for he is strong that executeth his word: for the day of the Lord is great and very terrible; and who can abide it?"—Joel 2:11.

"And I saw an angel standing in the sun; and he cried with a loud voice, saying to all the fowls that fly in the midst of heaven, Come and gather yourselves together unto the supper of the great God;

"That ye may eat the flesh of kings, and the flesh of captains, and the flesh of mighty men, and the flesh of horses, and of them that sit on them, and the flesh of all men, both free and bond, both small and great.

"And I saw the beast, and the kings of the earth, and their armies, gathered together to make war against him that sat on the horse, and against his army.

"And the beast was taken, and with him the false prophet that wrought miracles before him, with which he deceived them that had received the mark of the beast, and them that worshipped his image. These both were cast alive into a lake of fire burning with brimstone."—Rev. 19:17-20.

We have had about 275 years of peace out of the centuries of known world history. Since the fall of man in the Garden of Eden, man has been fighting and killing. Rebellion and bloodshed mark the course of man through the centuries.

There have been many great battles in the past years. The Bible tells us of many. Some were bloody; some were not. In Gideon's victory over Midian, the enemy fled. The victory was complete; the loss of life, nil.

Hezekiah also had a great victory over Sennacherib. The angel of the Lord smote 185,000 at one time. "And when they arose early in the morning, behold, they were all dead corpses" (II Kings 19:35).

But in most battles it has been man against man, and great have been the losses.

In the battle of Waterloo, between Napoleon and Wellington, each side lost about 2,400 men.

In the battle of Iwo Jima, the Americans lost over 4,000; and the Japanese, 20,000.

In 1944 at the battle of Normandy, the U. S. forces lost 8,975.

We deplore the loss of life and property through wicked wars. But at the same time, we must face the fact of other wars to come. War will never cease in this present age.

The *Detroit News* had an editorial entitled "Armageddon?" The first paragraph of the editorial read:

> Secretary of Defense McNamara reminded us the whole world lives on the edge of an abyss when he estimated that as many as 149 million Americans might lose their lives if the Soviet Union launched a nuclear attack upon the United States in the 1970s.

Mr. McNamara gave his estimate of the loss of life in case of a nuclear attack, based upon the weapons of this present day.

In a book written in 1938, I read about Mr. Frank Hales, writing from London, describing "Standing Death," the most terrible of all war weapons. He stated that this weapon was held secretly by France. He said that the French used the weapon only twice for purely experimental purposes. It cost the lives of thousands of Germans. The weapon was set aside in reserve. Today both France and Britain have in reserve this medium for wholesale death.

One paragraph of Mr. Hales' article said this:

One day in the early part of the war, a line of French soldiers moved catlike toward the German trenches a few thousand
feet ahead. They saw the German soldiers standing in their
trenches, their bayonets fixed—in deathly silence. The Germans
did not move. They were dead—more than 5,000 of them! There
were no wounds nor signs of poison gas. They were standing in
battle formation. The soldiers had been killed by the most power-
ful explosive ever handled by man. The inventor of it is Eugene
Turpin, born in 1846, the son of a Paris shoemaker.

Such an account is interesting, but we no longer hear much about
the use of an explosive invented back in 1937 or in the 19th century
by a Paris shoemaker.

Today man has developed much more. Because of modern arma-
ments, man moves cautiously, but strangely war still continues.

In the past forty years [preached in 1965], the nations of Europe
have signed over 200 peace treaties, and still war is threatening.

If Christ should come tonight—He can come at any time—
Christians will be caught up into the air to meet our Saviour.

*"For the Lord himself shall descend from heaven with a shout,
with the voice of the archangel, and with the trump of God: and the
dead in Christ shall rise first:*

*"Then we which are alive and remain shall be caught up together
with them in the clouds, to meet the Lord in the air: and so shall we
ever be with the Lord."*—I Thess. 4:16, 17.

But when the saved are caught up, the lost will be left on earth.
The Tribulation of seven years will begin. Three and one-half years
will be a time of intense suffering—war, bloodshed and death. The
book of the Revelation gives us accounts of that which is to come.

But now we come to Revelation 19:11-21. In this portion we have
a picture of the revelation of Christ (His coming in glory). We have
a picture of the Battle of Armageddon and the doom of the beast and
false prophet.

Spend a moment to review the coming of Christ. Look at Revelation 19:11-16. We see the heavens opened and the rider on the
white horse. More than 1,900 years ago the heavens opened to receive
Him. During this time He has been at the Father's right hand. Now,

Heaven's door swings wide open for His return to and for His rule over the earth. On His head are many crowns. His clothing is dipped in blood. The armies of Heaven follow Him, clothed in fine linen, white and clean. Out of the mouth of this One goes a sharp sword; and it is with this sword that He smites the nations.

We read in verse 16, "And he hath on his. . .thigh a name written, KING OF KINGS, AND LORD OF LORDS."

Look for a moment at the Battle of Armageddon. This battle will take place when Christ comes *with* His own. First the rapture, then the revelation, when Christ comes down to this earth and into this atmosphere. Then He will come for the battle against the beast and false prophet and their armies. This battle is called the Battle of Armageddon. "And he gathered them together into a place called in the Hebrew tongue Armageddon" (Rev. 16:16).

And now permit me to give you three very simple thoughts, easy to be remembered.

I. THE PLACE OF THE BATTLE

The battle will be fought in the valley of Megiddo, southeast of Mt. Carmel, in the land of Palestine.

The place without the city is "the valley of Jehoshaphat." We read in Joel 3:12, "Let the heathen be wakened, and come up to the valley of Jehoshaphat: for there will I sit to judge all the heathen round about."

It is also called the valley of decision in Joel 3:14. There will be fought the greatest decisive battle of all times. The contending parties will be on either side: on one side, the kings of the earth and the whole world (Rev. 16:14), under the beast and his armies, of which there will be multitudes; on the other side, the Lord Jesus Christ, the Lamb of God, now coming as King, riding upon a white horse.

A vision of Armageddon is given to us in Revelation:

"And the angel thrust in his sickle into the earth, and gathered the vine of the earth, and cast it into the great winepress of the wrath of God.

"And the winepress was trodden without the city, and blood came

out of the winepress, even unto the horse bridles, by the space of a thousand and six hundred furlongs."—Rev. 14:19, 20.

What a tragic and bloody scene is this!

II. THE PEOPLE OF THE BATTLE

"For they are the spirits of devils, working miracles, which go forth unto the kings of the earth and of the whole world, to gather them to the battle of that great day of God Almighty."—Rev. 16:14.

"Behold, the day of the Lord cometh, and thy spoil shall be divided in the midst of thee.

"For I will gather all nations against Jerusalem to battle; and the city shall be taken, and the houses rifled, and the women ravished; and half of the city shall go forth into captivity, and the residue of the people shall not be cut off from the city.

"Then shall the Lord go forth, and fight against those nations, as when he fought in the day of battle."—Zech. 14:1-3.

Yes, all nations of the earth will be concerned in the Battle of Armageddon.

The Bible pictures our Lord coming from Glory with His army to fight in this battle: "And the armies which were in heaven followed him upon white horses, clothed in fine linen, white and clean" (Rev. 19:14).

We are coming with our Lord to the Battle of Armageddon. This is fully established by a number of verses.

"To the end he may stablish your hearts unblameable in holiness before God, even our Father, at the coming of our Lord Jesus Christ with all his saints."—I Thess. 3:13.

"When Christ, who is our life, shall appear, then shall ye also appear with him in glory."—Col. 3:4.

"And Enoch also, the seventh from Adam, prophesied of these, saying, Behold, the Lord cometh with ten thousands of his saints."— Jude 14.

The Lord is coming to do battle with the nations of the earth. Give some thought to the Son of God. His eyes are as a flame of fire. He knows all things. There is nothing hidden or covered to Him with whom the world has to do. On His head are many crowns. He will be crowned because He is worthy. His crowns will be many because His reign covers every phase of every dominion.

His name is "the Word of God," this name given to Christ from the beginning, for "In the beginning was the Word, and the Word was with God, and the Word was God" (John 1:1). The eternity of the Word is a wonderful conception of truth. God's Word was not something hatched up by man nor something copied from some ancient writers. It is a Word forever settled in Heaven and given to men.

His name is KING OF KINGS, AND LORD OF LORDS, a name that carries with it all supremacy. He is the King over all kings. He is Lord over all. To Him every knee shall bow. He will reign over things temporal and political. He will also reign over things spiritual and priestly.

And what about the armies of this King of kings? The armies will be the saints who were raptured; as our Saviour comes down from the skies, they come with Him. He is riding a white horse, and they, too, will be riding upon white horses.

The saints will be clothed in linen, white and clean. Once again we are face to face with righteousness. Christ bears the name, "Faithful and True," for He wars in righteousness. We wear garments of linen, which, from the days of the tabernacle in the wilderness, have stood for righteousness. Everything about the Battle of Armageddon from the divine side is a warfare based on righteous judgment.

And the Word says that the saints will follow Him (Rev. 19:14). On the earth they follow Him; in Heaven they follow Him. On the earth they followed Him in His isolation, rejection and shame; now they follow Him in His glory, victory and power. What a wonderful honor to follow in the steps of our Lord!

III. THE PURPOSE OF THE BATTLE

1. *To exalt Christ, the "KING OF KINGS, AND LORD OF*

LORDS" (Rev. 19:16). The Saviour is worthy of all exaltation. This battle will be His battle. He will win with the sword that proceedeth out of His mouth. The Word of the Almighty God will be sufficient to subdue the enemies of our God.

2. *To put an end to satanic power.* The beast and the false prophet will be cast alive "into a lake of fire burning with brimstone." Satan will be cast into the bottomless pit and bound for a thousand years. What a glorious purpose for this Battle of Armageddon—the greatest battle of all history, when Satan is put down and all of his emissaries!

3. *To usher in the promised millennial reign.* The promise of the Word of God is that one day there will be a reign of God upon the earth, when war shall be no more.

"And he shall judge among the nations, and shall rebuke many people: and they shall beat their swords into plowshares, and their spears into pruninghooks: nation shall not lift up sword against nation, neither shall they learn war any more."—Isa. 2:4.

"They shall not hurt nor destroy in all my holy mountain: for the earth shall be full of the knowledge of the Lord, as the waters cover the sea."—Isa. 11:9.

"Blessed and holy is he that hath part in the first resurrection: on such the second death hath no power, but they shall be priests of God and of Christ, and shall reign with him a thousand years."—Rev. 20:6.

The Battle of Armageddon will usher in the millennial kingdom—the golden age. This is the time when Christ will reign, and we with Him.

4. *To set us in our appointed places.* We are children of the kingdom. The Bible says, "If we suffer, we shall also reign with him."

The Apostle Paul said to the church in Corinth, "Do ye not know that the saints shall judge the world? and if the world shall be judged by you, are ye unworthy to judge the smallest matters?" (I Cor. 6:2).

Yes, we have an appointed place in the kingdom of our Christ. To many He will say, "Well done, good and faithful servant; thou hast been faithful over a few things, I will make thee ruler over many things."

Eternal Heaven is not an empty, meaningless place. It begins with our rapture, continues through the one thousand years on earth, then extends into the eternity of the new Heaven and the new earth.

I like the verse in Joel 3:14, "Multitudes, multitudes in the valley of decision: for the day of the Lord is near in the valley of decision."

The day of the great battle will be a time of decision. It will be the most decisive battle of all the ages.

But there is something else to keep in mind. *This* is also a time of decision. It is a time when you must give an answer unto the Lord. You are saved or lost. You are condemned or not condemned. You are redeemed or not redeemed. It all depends on what you have done with the Saviour.

This is also the valley of death: "And as it is appointed unto men once to die, but after this the judgment." Death is on every hand. The sudden news of death may come to any of us at any time. The messenger of Death may speak to us at any second. Are you prepared to die? This Bible warns, "Prepare to meet thy God."

This is also the valley of deliverance. In Him we are delivered from the penalty and power of death and of Hell. In Him we have the promise of victory in our day-to-day living. In Him we can have the power of the Holy Spirit on us, directing us.

Give thought to the valley of decision, and make your decision now for Christ.

Remember that *this* is the valley of death. This is the time when lives are quickly snuffed out.

This is also the valley of deliverance. In Jesus we can have complete and eternal deliverance.

The Lord Jesus Christ is coming again! These precious words should thrill our hearts. The Lord is coming again! When we say this, the things of the world seem exceedingly small—its pomp and pride, its pleasure and pain, its praise and blame.

The Lord Jesus is coming again! These words should make us eager to bring our loved ones to Christ lest they be left behind at His coming.

A widely known Bible teacher said that there was a time when he was greatly interested in the second coming of Christ but that, of late, he had been so taken up with the glory of the indwelling Christ that he had lost interest in the thought of His return.

Such a person has turned away from much of the Bible, for the Bible speaks repeatedly of the return of our Saviour. And if we love the Lord, we will want to be ready to meet Him when He comes again.

Do you love His appearing? Are you endeavoring to get others ready for His coming?

14

Seven Words to Live By

"Wherewithal shall a young man cleanse his way? by taking heed thereto according to thy word.

"With my whole heart have I sought thee: O let me not wander from thy commandments.

"Thy word have I hid in mine heart, that I might not sin against thee.

"Blessed art thou, O Lord: teach me thy statutes.

"With my lips have I declared all the judgments of thy mouth.

"I have rejoiced in the way of thy testimonies, as much as in all riches.

"I will meditate in thy precepts, and have respect unto thy ways.

"I will delight myself in thy statutes: I will not forget thy word."—
Ps. 119:9–16.

Look back at verse 11, "Thy word [the proper word] have I hid in mine heart [the proper place], that I might not sin against thee." The Bible tells us that "faith cometh by hearing, and hearing by the word of God."

You have been taught in school the importance of God's Holy Word. Never get away from the fact that out of millions of books, this is the supreme, eternal Word of God given to us for now and for all the days to come—God's holy, holy Word.

I want to give you seven simple words to live by.

I. FAITH

Faith is a word to live by. In Mark 11:22 Jesus said, "Have faith in God." Faith, the faith that saves—Ephesians 2:8, 9: "For by grace are ye saved through faith; and that not of yourselves: it is the gift of God: Not of works, lest any man should boast." The faith that saves, a faith that you live, a faith that reigns in your heart and cheers you in the darkest hour—have faith in God!

I get sick and tired of all these whimpering, whining Christians. I meet them everywhere. Complaining, complaining. They act like God is dead. They are always finding fault. They are always hunting for a psychologist or a psychiatrist to help them. They can have all the help they need right here. I have nothing against men of their profession, but the Bible is all we need.

Build your faith on the Word of God. Read your Bible and believe it. Then build it on past experiences. Has God ever failed you? Not one single time. And He never will. Have you seen God do great things for others? Then He will do great things for you.

II. OBEDIENCE

Put this verse alongside *obedience:* "If ye love me, keep my commandments." Then we read, "Behold, to obey is better than sacrifice, and to hearken than the fat of rams" (I Sam. 15:22).

1. *Obey the Lord in baptism.* You are saved by faith in Christ, but your baptism is an act of obedience.

2. *Obey the Lord in worship at the house of God.* A motto I have used for years and years is: THREE TO THRIVE—Sunday morning, Sunday night and Wednesday night. I have never known a man to backslide who attended church these three times weekly. There may be one, but I have never met him—not in our church. God will bless those who regularly come to His house. They will make things right with others and get going for God in winning souls. That is obedience. That is an act of doing something.

I go to churches where they have great crowds on Sunday morning. Then on Sunday night, twenty-five, thirty, or forty people are present. I don't go for that kind of stuff. Just plain turning away from God's house and refusing to worship Him—that is not God's way. You obey the Lord.

3. *Obey the Lord in tithing.* Every Christian should be a tither. "Bring ye all the tithes into the storehouse, that there may be meat in mine house, and prove me now herewith, saith the Lord of hosts, if I will not open you the windows of heaven, and pour you out a blessing, that there shall not be room enough to receive it" (Mal. 3:10).

Trust God. Have faith in God. God never fails. He will supply your needs. Be a faithful tither of your income and claim the promise that He will open the windows of Heaven and pour you out a blessing that there shall not be room enough to receive.

4. *Obey Him in witnessing.* "Ye shall be witnesses unto me" (Acts 1:8).

Obedience—hang onto it. What an important word it is!

III. CONSECRATION

The third word is *consecration.*

"I beseech you therefore, brethren, by the mercies of God, that ye present your bodies a living sacrifice, holy, acceptable unto God, which is your reasonable service.

"And be not conformed to this world: but be ye transformed by the renewing of your mind, that ye may prove what is that good, and acceptable, and perfect, will of God."—Rom. 12:1, 2.

Separation from the world is living for Christ every day, every hour, turning away from evil and wrongdoing and resting wholly and completely on Him. "Wherefore come out from among them, and be ye separate, saith the Lord, and touch not the unclean thing; and I will receive you" (II Cor. 6:17).

Don't worry about being *too* separated. That is not our danger. Some people are afraid of being too good. The Devil will take care of that, and the flesh will, too.

Now I hope you will say, "I'm going to live a completely separated life." That means you are giving everything to Him, laying all on the altar. That means you have the fullness of the Holy Spirit, which comes by emptiness and willingness. Be empty of self and willing for God to fill you.

Then you want to die to self. Paul said in I Corinthians 15:31, "I die daily." That is where troubles come from, where we have conflicts in the church, in the home, in the school and elsewhere. Choir members, ushers, deacons, get that self item out of there! Be willing to die daily. Desire a life of consecration to God, giving everything to Him.

IV. SERVICE

Let me give you some verses to go along with *service.* Mark 10:43, 44:

"But so shall it not be among you: but whosoever will be great among you, shall be your minister:

"And whosoever of you will be the chiefest, shall be servant of all."

Oh, but you don't want to be a servant. You want to be a boss, a big shot. The Lord Jesus was a servant. And to be Christlike, one has to be a servant, too. A servant seeks no big, high place.

To you graduates I say, take any place offered you. Be willing to be a servant. If you can serve God, serve Him. Don't ask for some big place, some big spot, a big salary. Leave that to God. You just be His servant! God is calling for servants.

We have lost that word today. We don't have service stations now. We run and put our gas in, then run and pay the girl at the window, and that is it. We pump up our own tires and wipe off our own windshields. Service is gone!

But you be willing to be a servant. If God is putting His hand upon you young people for Christian service, then serve Him with all your heart. The greatest honor that can come to you is to be His servant—a preacher, a missionary, a Christian teacher. Serve Him with all your heart. Put away your pride and be a servant.

I just came from preaching in Atlanta where I held two nights of meetings. They were beautiful services. I couldn't help but think of them. I drove right by the federal penitentiary in Atlanta.

When I was called to preach, I was eighteen years old. The pastor preached, and I walked down the aisle and said, "I believe God has called me to preach." I didn't know all about it, and I was scared half to death, but I believed He had called me.

The pastor had me stand right in the front. He said, "While this young man stands here, if other young men feel called to preach, come and stand with him." And to my surprise, eight young men came. There were nine of us standing there. One person came by, took my hand and shook it. Another came and whispered in my ear, "Son, if God has called you, don't you dare do anything else. I was your age when God called me. I turned away from His call and took a job to make money. I have made money, but I have never been happy." I have never forgotten that advice.

Nine of us were standing in line. But out of the nine, I am the only one who preached. The rest turned away.

The boy by my right side was named Emmons. He passed his thirtieth birthday, went down back of his house, took a 22 rifle and killed himself. All the others have passed away except one. The boy on my left side was named Miller. He is occupying a cell in the federal penitentiary in Atlanta, Georgia, right now. He is now eighty-three. I am a year older. Isn't that awful! All of them failed completely!

My dear young people, if God has called you into His service, don't you dare do anything else. Do what God says! It may be to preach to a little handful or to talk to one person or to serve on some mission field. Wherever it may be, you say, "Lord, I'm willing to be Your servant."

V. WATCHFULNESS

I will give you a verse to go alongside *watchfulness*. Write down Matthew 25:13: "Watch therefore, for ye know neither the day nor the hour wherein the Son of man cometh."

Watch! Christ said, "I will come again." The second coming is mentioned in the Bible some fifteen hundred times. One verse in every twenty in the New Testament refers to the return of Jesus. He is coming! And when He comes, the dead in Christ shall be raised, the living shall be changed, and together we shall be caught up in the air to meet our blessed Lord.

Coming! That is a word to live by. Don't let that be far from your mind, because He may come at any moment. We have no promise of another day, another hour. His coming is imminent. It is hanging over us. At any moment He may come and receive us up into His presence, to be with Him forevermore. Let the second coming change your life.

Live! Live every day as though the next moment you will stand in His presence. Live, watch, the second coming—keep these in mind. They will help you understand your Bible, help you in daily living with your family, and make you a soul winner.

VI. COMPASSION

For that single word *compassion,* I want to give you a Scripture that will go alongside it with all of its beauty. Write down Matthew 9:36: "But when he saw the multitudes, he was moved with compassion on them, because they fainted, and were scattered abroad, as sheep having no shepherd."

Would you like to be Christlike? Then have compassion. This is a tough old world. We are mean men. We are tough. We are money crazy. We are property crazy. We are appearance crazy. We don't much care. We rush on our way. We are not concerned about others. We have no compassion!

I talked to a pastor the other day who is giving up his buses. He said, "We just got tired of hauling those kids into the church." I have never gotten tired of busing people. I wish we had twice as many buses as we have now—thirty-five.

Compassion! Love folks. Have the compassion of our Saviour. Jesus cared! We, too, must care.

Sometime when your heart gets hard, when you get a little thoughtless about other people, then say, "Lord, give me compassion to love folks." Love them when they are unkind, when they say things they shouldn't say. In compassion, love them, pray for them, go out of your way to help them.

I preached up in Middle Tennessee the other day. When I gave the invitation I said, "If some of you want to be soul winners, then why don't you come forward?" Quite a group came and stood around the altar. I finished up the service.

The second night I stood up and began reading the Bible to begin the service. The back door opened. A man and a woman, perhaps in their fifties, walked in. They stood there at the door. Right away I saw that they had a little problem. He wanted to sit on the back row, and she wanted to come up front. They were having a little discussion. He tried to pull her in that back row. She motioned "no" and pulled him towards the front. They kept that up for a few minutes and were disturbing my Bible reading.

I was interested to see who was going to win. Lo and behold, she did! She brought him down the aisle, and they sat on the second row. She got in first, and he came and sat next to her, right on the end.

I never saw a more unhappy man. He wanted to be on the back row so he could get out fast, but there he was sitting on the second row. He looked at me as if he could kill me.

I preached, then gave an invitation. God blessed, and numbers of people came forward to be saved. Then at the end of the service I said, "Before we go, I would like to ask if there is somebody else here who would like to be saved." To my shocking surprise, the fellow on the second row raised his hand. He had been mad through the whole service, I thought, but he had listened.

I said, "Sir, you want to be saved?"

"Yes, I do."

"Then come out of your seat and up to the front."

He came, and I directed him to a man who took him over to one side and led him to the Lord.

He came back in a few moments wiping away the tears and saying, "Praise God! I hadn't been to church in thirty-two years; and the first time I came, I got saved!"

I looked down at the little lady who came with him in that door. She was standing there with a beautiful smile on her face. I thought, *I better go and speak to her and tell her how happy I am that her husband got saved.*

I put out my hand and said, "Ma'am, I know that you're glad your husband got saved." She didn't move. I thought she must not have heard me, so I got a little louder. "I know you're glad that your husband got saved tonight." She still didn't move. I thought, *Here is a strange case.*

About that time a lady came up and whispered in my ear, "Brother Roberson, that's her brother, not her husband. He hasn't been home in years. The reason she's not shaking hands with you is that she's totally blind. But she came forward in church last night and said, 'Though I'm blind, I want to win someone to the Lord.' Then on Tuesday morning, in walked her brother. She latched onto him. She said, 'You can't get away without going to church.' He said, 'I haven't gone in thirty-two years, and I'm not going now.' She said, 'Yes, you are!' And she stayed with him all day long and brought him to church tonight."

God saved him. I saw the man baptized. He is now living for Christ and serving God faithfully.

All of it goes back to the compassion of the little blind sister. She cared, and something happened because she cared.

VII. FAITHFULNESS

Faithfulness. Write down beside that I Corinthians 4:2: "Moreover it is required in stewards, that a man be found faithful." The Bible says, "Well done, thou good and faithful servant." The Bible says, "Be thou faithful unto death, and I will give thee a crown of life."

Faithfulness is mentioned thoughout the Bible. We may be physically unable to do certain things, but we can be faithful. We may not be educated to the place where we can do some things, but we can be faithful. We may be limited in money, but we can be faithful. Determine to be a faithful servant for God.

I made a promise to God when I got saved at age fourteen. Nobody asked me to. I just decided that was what I wanted: "I'll never miss a service in church for the rest of my life unless I'm ill." I am now almost eighty-five, and I have not missed a service since I was fourteen, except when I was in the hospital—neither Sunday morning, Sunday night, nor Wednesday night. I have been overseas, I have been around the world, but I have not missed a service.

I promised God, "I'll give a tithe all my life," and I have. God has kept His Word to me, and I have kept my promise to Him.

I promised God to read the Bible every day, and I have done it for all these years. And I have prayed every day.

On this matter of faithfulness, so many are up and down, in and out, off and on. Be faithful! Be steadfast! Do the job and be someone on whom others can depend.

Seven words to live by—as simple as they can be, but they will work in your life if you let them.

When God speaks to you young folks, you obey. God has a will for your life, and He wants you to be in His will. God will empower you by the Holy Spirit for any task that He wants you to do. Now, you say to Him, "Lord, just whisper Your will to me." You can hear the voice of God; then say, "Dear Lord, I'm ready—ready to obey You and ready to do what You say."

Part II
Leadership Thoughts and Ideas

*used in hundreds of churches
to encourage soul winning, visitation
and the building of great Sunday schools*

15

Building a
Great Church

Consider the title of this chapter, "Building a Great Church." I didn't say "building a *large* church"—some large churches are far from great. I am not primarily concerned about bigness in numbers and finances, but I am concerned about "greatness." Let the local church be great in spirit, great in concern, great in missionary outlook, great in work, and especially great in soul winning.

I have seen great churches in rural communities, small towns and mission fields—churches great in spirit, attitudes and accomplishments.

Leadership is the key. Everything rises and falls on leadership. The pastor is to be a leader. Normally, the church will do no more than the pastor wishes or does. The pastor who wants his work to go forward must give himself to his task.

For more than fifty-five years I have been declaring, "Everything rises or falls on leadership." Original? I don't know. It has been a part of my thinking for a long time. And it is true! Leadership is the key to success and victory. Failure comes when leadership fails.

Nations fail because of leadership. A study of Israel shows this. King Saul and King Solomon illustrate this truth. The kings of the northern and southern kingdoms picture it vividly. But in every age, yes, in this twentieth century, nations rise and fall on leadership.

States, countries and cities fail when leadership fails. Churches fail when leadership fails. The pastor, God's leader for the local church, must do right, or the work will fail. Sunday school classes fail with poor leadership. Youth work fails, missionary enterprises fail with weak leadership.

But with the right leadership, miracles take place.

I have seen abandoned churches reopened, revitalized, revived and restored to great usefulness. I have seen dwindling Sunday school classes catch fire, begin to grow and reach scores of people when the proper leader was found. I have seen churches and Sunday schools touch an entire city when the power of God moved through dedicated leaders.

This is a very informal book. I speak out of my heart. I want to "sum up" my sixty-six years in the ministry. I want to go back to my home church near Louisville, Kentucky, where I made my profession of faith in Christ, followed the Lord in believer's baptism, and where I learned my first lesson in building a successful work. My pastor, Rev. J. N. Binford, was my teacher. The church was not large; but it was aggressive, active and Bible-centered. The pastor believed in organization and being faithful to Christ. I worked with him; I saw his zeal and compassion.

My first full-time work was at the Virginia Avenue Baptist Church of Louisville. My pastor was L. W. Benedict from New York State, a graduate of the Southern Baptist seminary. There is where I got my first lesson on the importance of visitation. Brother Benedict kept me visiting night and day, covering the west end of Louisville.

In addition to visitation, I directed the church music. I worked at the church's radio station, WLAP (We Love All People). I taught a Sunday school class (all of this before I was twenty). At the same time, I attended school at the University of Louisville and took some classes at the Southern Baptist seminary. (My salary was $40.00 per month. This was in the Depression days.)

My first pastorate was at the Germantown Baptist Church, located at the edge of Memphis, Tennessee. This church called me. Virginia Avenue Baptist Church ordained me. The ordination sermon in 1932 was by my first pastor, Rev. J. N. Binford.

Thirty-two people were present on my first Sunday morning at Germantown. The church was organized about 1865. The building was old but beautiful. I remained at my first church one year. There I baptized many converts. There we built a Sunday school building and filled it with happy people, young and old.

In my first full-time work as pastor, I visited constantly. We organized the Sunday school. We grew.

And then, a big mistake! I stepped out of the will of God. Without prayer and meditation, I accepted the position of assistant pastor of the Temple Baptist Church in Memphis. I experienced three months of misery. Soon after taking the position, I knew I was out of God's will. The pastor insisted that I stay, but I had to leave.

Then followed five months of emptiness—no church, no work.

Then I was invited to speak at the Greenbrier Baptist Church, Greenbrier, Tennessee, twenty-two miles from Nashville. The little church called me. This time I waited on God. I prayed earnestly. The Lord directed me to take the church. I spent three happy years there as pastor. I lived in a tiny room at the back of the church. There was no bathroom, no telephone—just one room; but I was happy, for I was in His will.

In 1935 I was called to be the evangelist for the Birmingham Baptist Association. I was elected by the association. I received no salary but love offerings from my meetings. I preached fifty-five revivals in churches and tents and enjoyed a great season of soul winning for two years.

In 1937 I was called to pastor the First Baptist Church of Fairfield, Alabama, adjoining Birmingham. That year I got married! I entered the work of the pastorate again. For five years we worked with the Fairfield church. It grew from 125 to an average of 850. Evangelism, both public and private, was pushed. The Sunday school was expanded. There was growth in every division of the work. We were very happy.

But one Sunday a pulpit committee appeared from Chattanooga. The Highland Park Baptist Church there had endeavored to get Dr. John C. Cowell of the Central Baptist Church of Decatur,

Alabama, to be their pastor; but when he refused their offer, he gave the committee my name.

The committee heard me preach and invited me to Highland Park for a service. I did visit the church for one Sunday morning in October of 1942. The church called me, but I was not sure of God's will. I waited. I prayed. Dr. T. W. Callaway of Chattanooga came to see me to add his emphasis to the call.

It was a struggle, but I finally knew the will of God and accepted the call. I knew it was God's will. I never doubted this.

This pastorate lasted forty years and six months. Oh, what miraculous, wonderful things took place in over four decades!

First and foremost the soul-winning program began at once. Sunday after Sunday people walked the aisles. There were souls saved every Sunday for forty years and six months.

The Sunday school began to grow! From a few score in Sunday school, the attendance went to many thousands. The people were faithful and responsive.

The visitation program started and continued without abatement. Evangelism was emphasized.

From the church auditorium (now Phillips Chapel) we moved to a sawdust-floor tabernacle, spending four years in that rough building. It was hot in the summer and cold in the winter. Next, we built the tabernacle (now Chauncey-Goode Auditorium) which seated about 2,500. We continued to grow, so we expanded the balcony and sides of the tabernacle to seat 3,500. This building was used for all services from 1947 to 1981.

The big tabernacle seating 6,000 was constructed and put in use in September, 1981.

From the beginning at Highland Park, the midweek service was the center of our work. We placed great emphasis on the Wednesday prayer service—"The Sweetest Service of the Week." Our motto, THREE TO THRIVE, came into being—Sunday morning, Sunday evening and Wednesday. At the prayer service, we had the choir and orchestra in place. There was a song service, with perhaps two specials and a season of prayer. A prayer list was mimeographed and given to the people, listing the sick in hospitals and homes, the shut-ins, the bereaved and a few of our 560 missionaries. Two or three men were called to the platform to lead in prayer.

An offering for missions was received each Wednesday. The people gave generously.

In every service, a message was given, followed by an invitation.

16

"Everything Rises and Falls on Leadership"

What Makes a Great Christian Leader?

1. *Salvation* is first and of primary importance. A leader in Christian work must definitely know he is saved. He must be able to say with the Apostle Paul, "For the which cause I also suffer these things: nevertheless I am not ashamed: for I know whom I have believed, and am persuaded that he is able to keep that which I have committed unto him against that day" (II Tim. 1:12).

Yes, the leader in Christian work must have knowledge of his salvation and must manifest that he is saved by the way he walks, talks and lives.

2. *Dedication.* We will never achieve much nor be found faithful unless there is a wholehearted dedication to our Lord, a dedication to His Word, and a dedication to His work.

3. *Daring.* The leader must not be afraid to "launch out into the deep." The record of men in the past who accomplished much for our Lord shows that they were daring, that they launched out and moved forward. Paul was daring. A study of the lives of Wesley, Whitefield, Spurgeon, Moody, and others shows their daring quality.

4. *Diplomacy,* the ability to handle people. Never compromise but understand how to work with others. Leaders must know how to be diplomatic. Remember this: don't make trouble, handle trouble! Be firm but diplomatic. Be considerate of others.

5. *Determination.* Paul declared:

"Brethren, I count not myself to have apprehended: but this one thing I do, forgetting those things which are behind, and reaching forth unto those things which are before, I press toward the mark for the prize of the high calling of God in Christ Jesus."—Phil. 3:13, 14.

Paul was not a quitter! He went forward in spite of all the persecution, suffering and opposition. To achieve in this field of work, we must have such determination.

6. *Death.* Paul said, "I die daily." Paul said, "Now if we be dead with Christ, we believe that we shall also live with him."

This great verse that has meant so much in my life is John 12:24, "Verily, verily, I say unto you, Except a corn of wheat fall into the ground and die, it abideth alone: but if it die, it bringeth forth much fruit."

A leader of others in Christian work must reckon self to be dead. We must not be turned away from a determination to follow Christ by the minor things of life. We must die to them and victoriously march on with our Lord.

7. *Direction.* Great Christians always seek God's direction. They do not move out blindly but wait on Him and seek His guidance.

Study your Bible carefully. Notice the guidance given to Abraham, Moses, Joshua, Daniel and others. Be sure of God's guidance. If there is some uncertainty, wait for direction.

We find guidance in three ways: by a study of His Word, by fervent prayer, by obedience to His plain commands.

17

Christian
Leadership

I have no interest in building leadership ability of unbelievers. I am deeply concerned for God's work and the building of leadership for Christian work.

A place to begin is with the master Leader, the Lord Jesus Christ. We make no mistakes when we walk in His steps.

For many years my life text was I Peter 2:21, "For even hereunto were ye called; because Christ also suffered for us, leaving us an example, that ye should follow his steps."

How deeply and carefully do I urge you to study the life and work of our Saviour! He was perfect and gives us perfect examples. Study His life of prayer and fellowship with His Father. Study His attitude toward critics and toward those who sought His life. Study His life of concern for others. The blind, the lame, the poor, the hated were all recipients of His divine favor.

In the study of leadership, keep close to the Saviour.

I. HAVE FAITH IN GOD

Faith keeps us moving forward when all seems against us. Faith gives courage against tremendous odds.

1. *Build your faith by studying Christ.* Read where He said, "Have

faith in God" (Mark 11:22). Determine to follow Him. Ask yourself, "What would Jesus do?"

2. *Build your faith by studying the Bible.* Read, study and rely on the promises of God. Believe the Word! Believe every promise. Remember Christ said, "For with God nothing shall be impossible."

3. *Build your faith by studying other men of faith.* Study Hebrews 11, the great "faith chapter." "By faith Abel..."; "By faith Enoch..."; "By faith Noah..."; "By faith Abraham...." Not only can you build your faith by studying these Bible characters, but you can build it by studying those since Bible days who have excelled in faith.

II. BE DEAD TO SELF AND BE FILLED WITH THE SPIRIT

"Verily, verily, I say unto you, Except a corn of wheat fall into the ground and die, it abideth alone: but if it die, it bringeth forth much fruit."—John 12:24.

"Likewise reckon ye also yourselves to be dead indeed unto sin, but alive unto God through Jesus Christ our Lord."—Rom. 6:11.

"For ye are dead, and your life is hid with Christ in God."—Col. 3:3.

"And be not drunk with wine, wherein is excess; but be filled with the Spirit."—Eph. 5:18.

Christ is our noble example. He was dead to the flesh and filled with the Spirit. He told us to die to self and be filled with the Holy Spirit.

Self is your greatest enemy. Self defeats victorious living. Self brings weakness in battle.

"The fullness of the Spirit" brings power. Therefore, Christian, empty self and be filled with the Holy Spirit.

III. BE UNSELFISH

We have touched on part of this in the previous point, but I feel a necessity to emphasize unselfishness.

Christian, don't be concerned for what you can get for yourself or what honor it might bring to your own name.

Seeking money is the theme of the world everywhere. Even preachers, teachers, evangelists and missionaries are in danger of asking, "How much?"

The world seeks for position and things. How tragic when Christian leaders fall in line with the world! So many seek the big place and place of renown.

My first year in the ministry was at a little church in Germantown, Tennessee. Then came an invitation to be an assistant pastor at the Temple Baptist Church of Memphis. I looked at the bigness of the job, increase in salary, and foolishly accepted the position. At once I knew I was out of the will of God and resigned after the first month but stayed on under the teaching of the pastor. I resigned after the second month, but people urged me to stay and continue my work. At the end of the third month, I made my complete break. I was out of the will of God. I knew that, to be properly used, I must be in His will.

I say to all leaders, be Christlike, be unselfish.

IV. BE COURAGEOUS

The Lord spoke to Joshua, "Only be thou strong and very courageous." All Christian work takes courage! The world, the flesh and the Devil fight against us. It takes courage to stand against these three. Study again the courage of Moses, Elijah, Daniel. Study again the courage of Stephen, Paul, John and others.

V. HAVE DETERMINATION

Paul said:

"Brethren, I count not myself to have apprehended: but this one thing I do, forgetting those things which are behind, and reaching forth unto those things which are before, I press toward the mark for the prize of the high calling of God in Christ Jesus."—Phil. 3:13, 14.

The world is filled with quitters! "A winner never quits, and a quitter never wins."

Determine to do His will. God has a will for every person. Know that will and do it.

Determine to go forward despite all odds. Paul continued in spite of imprisonment, stoning by mobs, beatings, unfaithful workers and a weak body.

Determine to fight on to the end of your ministry. Paul could say, "I have fought a good fight, I have finished my course, I have kept the faith."

VI. BE COMPASSIONATE

Need I repeat that Christ cared? In Matthew 9:36 we read, "But when he saw the multitudes, he was moved with compassion on them, because they fainted, and were scattered abroad, as sheep having no shepherd."

A leader may not be super-intelligent, but he must be compassionate. A leader may not be highly educated, but he must be compassionate. A leader may not be a talented speaker, but he must be compassionate. A leader may not have a glowing, persuasive personality, but he must be compassionate.

18

The Essentials for
a Live, Aggressive,
Soul-winning Church

I was pastor of this kind of church for more than forty years. In addition, I have preached in hundreds of churches—some live, aggressive, soul-winning churches, and some not.

It has been my observation that greatness is not in finances nor in buildings. It is not in organization and education. Neither is it in music nor personalities.

Then what makes a church alive and aggressive?

1. *The preaching and teaching of the Word of God.* This must be the center of all of our work. Read the Word, obey the Word, preach the Word. Give it from the pulpit, from the Sunday school classrooms, in youth meetings. The Bible is our central Book: it has everything we need for victorious living.

2. *Three great evangelistic hours each week.* Sunday morning, Sunday evening and Wednesday evening—every service has a purpose, and that is to win people to Christ and to help Christians live established and fruitful lives of service. Evangelism is the center of all we do.

3. *Dependence on prayer power.* Great churches are praying churches! This means personal praying by the members. It means

praying together in the prayer services. It means relying on God for guidance and results. The need of every church is for a great midweek service!

4. *Separation from the world.* Hate sin! An individual must hate it, and the church must hate it. This is the day of low standards, of wickedness and carelessness, of shame and debauchery. A soul-winning church will be separated from the world.

5. *The fullness of the Spirit.* "Be filled with the Spirit." A soul-winning church is Spirit-led. Her people must be empty of self and be willing for God to use them. The Holy Spirit indwells each believer when he is completely surrendered.

6. *The truth of the second coming.* The live, aggressive, soul-winning church is ever looking for the return of Christ. He said, "I will come again." That He may come at any hour should inspire us to eager service, dedicated living and constant watching.

7. *Constant building of concern.* Do you have the concern of our Saviour, who "saw the multitudes, [and] he was moved with compassion on them"? Do you have the compassion of the Apostle Paul who said, "I have great heaviness and continual sorrow in my heart. For I could wish that myself were accursed from Christ for my brethren, my kinsmen according to the flesh"? Hour by hour do you manifest a concern for others? A God-blessed church must be compassionate. We must see a lost world and seek to win all we can. This means soul winning at home and missions to the ends of the earth.

19

A Live Church

A "live church" has a born-again pastor, a man who is saved and knows it. He is separated from the world and dedicated to his task.

A "live church" has a great and growing Sunday school, headed by an alert, Spirit-filled superintendent and teachers who love Christ and are dedicated to teaching others.

A "live church" has a wide-awake, faithful choir and a dedicated leader. The choir sings with the Spirit and with understanding.

A "live church" has a wide-awake corps of ushers, men dedicated and trained and faithful in their position of service. To be an usher in a large or small church is of great importance. Visitors are to be treated with respect. Members are to be welcomed with care.

A "live church" has an aggressive, evangelistic spirit Sunday morning, Sunday evening and Wednesday evening. Evangelism is the key spirit.

A "live church" has a dedicated board of deacons. There are only two offices in a New Testament church—the pastor and the deacons. They must be Spirit-filled men.

A "live church" has a thorough visitation program, a visitation program scheduled weekly to win people to Christ and to encourage the wayward and to reach out into every part of the city or community.

A "live church" has a continual burden for souls. Most churches have lost this. In America literally thousands of churches never see a single profession of faith. Why? They have lost the passion for souls.

20

Everything Is
Important

Some leaders are guilty of emphasizing certain matters of Christian service. But to the child of God, to the leader especially, *everything is important.*

1. *Every service.* For many years my motto to my people was: THREE TO THRIVE. In this I was emphasizing the importance of Sunday morning, Sunday evening and Wednesday evening. To a good leader, every service is of unique importance. We give attention to every hour.

2. *The bulletin.* Through the years I have had placed in my hands literally thousands of church bulletins, bulletins from our own church and from churches across the nation. Some are completely empty of anything of interest. They present no challenge, give no news.

A church bulletin, given out to the people in the Sunday morning hour, should contain vital announcements: the services of the church attractively presented; progress noted; opportunities presented. The bulletin is vital information to every member and should present a challenge to every Christian.

3. *The music.* I speak of all music. Congregational singing and specials should be carefully selected and prayerfully given. Let every song have a message of importance to everyone. Much of our

present-day music is lacking both in message and melody. Let every song lift up Christ. Let every song be a testimony of the heart and a mode of thanksgiving.

The song leader or music director ought to be a man of wisdom and prayer—Spirit-filled.

4. *The announcements.* Announcements are important! Give them thoroughly but briefly. Announcements are repeated again and again. I urge pastor and leaders to give study as to how to make your announcements attractive and effective.

5. *The preaching.* Preaching is important! It should be scriptural, interesting, informative, evangelistic. The goal of preaching is to inform people and to move their hearts toward obedience to God and His will.

6. *The invitation.* The invitation at the close of every service is of vital importance. I believe in invitations, both to saints and sinners. I believe in invitations for Christians to surrender themselves to the will of God. I believe in invitations to the unsaved to repent and to accept Christ as Saviour. The invitation is important and must be given prayerfully and expectantly.

7. *The reception of members.* When people respond to an invitation, it is an indication of their interest, their concern, their desire to let God rule in their lives. People who come forward during the invitation to be saved should be dealt with thoroughly. People who come to unite with the church should feel the warmth and concern of the membership.

Give a great welcome to all who come to unite with the church in any service. Every decision for Christ is important!

Ten Commandments for Church Leaders

THOU SHALT accept thy place of service, believing that God needs you where you are.

THOU SHALT do thy very best—not thy second best.

THOU SHALT seek to learn thy job and understand what it involves.

THOU SHALT be faithful to the services of thy church and to thy God-called, church-elected responsibility.

THOU SHALT study the Word of God and spend time in prayer each day.

THOU SHALT pray for the lost and seek to lead them to Christ.

THOU SHALT speak well of thy church and joyfully lead others to do likewise.

THOU SHALT work with the entire program of the church and cooperate with the pastor and staff, as well as other leaders.

THOU SHALT follow God's plan of Christian stewardship.

THOU SHALT seek the leadership of God in all matters and follow that leadership above all else.

—Copied

21

Seven Essentials for a Successful Visitation Program

Every Christian's desire should be to give the Gospel to as many people as possible. The church is to "go...into all the world, and preach the gospel." The goal of the Sunday school is to reach everyone possible with the good news of salvation.

For a successful visitation program, there must be:

★ A BURDEN FOR SOULS

We are to have the concern of our Saviour: "When he saw the multitudes, he was moved with compassion on them, because they fainted, and were scattered abroad, as sheep having no shepherd" (Matt. 9:36).

Keep before you the truth that men without Christ are lost. Therefore, give the Gospel to everyone you can. "All have sinned, and come short of the glory of God." All men need Christ as Saviour. To reach others, you must have a burden for them, a concern, a driving passion that sends you out to give them the message and to urge them to accept Christ.

★ A THOROUGH SURVEY

For a successful visitation program, you need names and addresses of people to visit. This is best acquired by doing a survey in your community. In this survey, get the names and addresses of all of the unchurched and all the unenlisted Baptists you can. A good survey will result in names of those who have never been invited to come to Christ or even invited to attend Sunday school.

Church members can be sent out at a designated time, going from door to door, and quietly and lovingly getting the names of those considered to be prospects for the Sunday school. Better still, there are fine Christian men who can be employed to take a survey of your community. They will go from door to door and will produce hundreds of prospects for the Sunday school.

A survey is important in order to build a Sunday school and win many to the Saviour.

★ A PLANNED VISITATION TIME

In the Highland Park Baptist Church, Chattanooga, where I served for forty years and six months, the visitation program was on every Thursday evening at six o'clock. Our people met, enjoyed a brief meal, then went out to visit absentees of the Sunday school and to get prospects for their classes. This visitation program can be both successful and enjoyable if done properly.

★ A VISITATION SECRETARY

Every church needs someone to keep records. You need a file of prospects for the Sunday school, both of the unsaved and the unchurched. This file is kept up-to-date by this designated person. From the file, names are taken and given to Christians going out on visitation. The visitation secretary can be a volunteer who is willing to give of her time to keep the records and to present names of prospects weekly.

★ A PLAN TO GET WORKERS

I am referring now to a plan to get workers for the regular visitation hour. At Highland Park, our plan was to get them on Wednesday evening at the prayer service. In the early part of every prayer meeting, I would say a few words about visitation and the importance of reaching people. I would ask all who would go visiting with us on Thursday evening at six o'clock to stand. An usher would hand a card to each one standing. The card would read, "I will be present for the visitation program Thursday evening at six o'clock."

By giving out the cards, we knew how many would be present and how many to prepare for.

Visitation is often a difficult task. From time to time, people have to be stirred to a new devotion to this work.

★ INSTRUCTION IN VISITATION

From week to week give instructions to those going out on visitation; instruction on how to dress, how to speak, and the manner of their behavior in homes they visit.

For instance, those going out on regular visitation should always be dressed properly. They must conduct themselves as Christians. Foolishness and frivolity have no part in this important task. People are instructed on how to knock on the door and what to say when people answer the door. They are instructed how to come to the point and how to deal quietly and definitely with their prospect.

Always visit for results, but be careful to let the Holy Spirit work through you.

★ PERSISTENCE!

In a successful visitation program, we must keep at it! In visiting the family without any church affiliation, we don't always get results on the first visit, so we go back again and again. We are not to get weary in repeating our calls. We are to strive to be kind and gracious so that even the unsaved and unenlisted will welcome us.

Always be kind and gracious and manifest the proper attitude toward the people you visit.

These are some of the essentials for a successful visitation program. You may wish to add others.

Get a survey of your community and begin at once to visit, write letters, and pray about reaching people for Christ.

22

Seven Essentials for a Growing Sunday School

This outline has been given in hundreds of churches and has been followed by many with amazing results.

★ BELIEVE IN THE WORD OF GOD

This is the first essential and perhaps the most important. Sunday school is a teaching organization. We are teaching the holy Word of God, God's infallible Book. Teachers, you must know this in presenting the Word of God and in giving the way of salvation and victorious living. Teachers, give out the Word!

★ A BURDEN FOR SOULS

This is a "MUST" for a growing Sunday school. Be concerned for others. Without this concern, we are nothing more than a worldly organization striving for worldly results. Men without Christ are lost! Believe this; then consistently give out the message of salvation in your Sunday school classes, young and old.

★ STANDARDS FOR TEACHERS

The Sunday schoolteacher is somebody special! He or she is superior to the doctor of philosophy in a big university. You are dealing with eternal Truth, so your position is superior to any other teaching position in the world.

Now, what are the standards for teachers?

1. *Salvation.* That means they must be born again. They are new creatures in Christ and members of the family of God. The first and most important standard for a teacher is his salvation.

2. *Separation.* Every teacher has an influence. 'No one lives to himself, and no one dies to himself.' Teachers are to live so that students can follow them in the right direction. Therefore, you teachers, be separated from the world and free from all entangling alliances that would hinder or hamper your influence. You cannot engage in worldly activities. You cannot participate in nor sponsor sinful pursuits.

3. *Faithfulness.* "Moreover it is required in stewards, that a man be found faithful"—faithful in church attendance on Sunday morning, Sunday evening and Wednesday evening; faithful in visitation; faithful in witnessing; faithful in Bible study and prayer.

4. *Loyalty*—first, loyal to the Lord Jesus Christ and the Word of God; second, loyal to the local church and to the pastor and the work of the church. Your loyalty must be unquestioned. You are not to be critics but builders.

★ A WEEKLY MEETING OF TEACHERS AND OFFICERS

To have a growing Sunday school, set a time each week when the pastor, the teachers and the officers meet together for discussion of the work of the Sunday school. Give the record of the past Sunday and plan for future Sundays.

This can be an exciting thirty-minute time each week. I prefer this meeting before the Wednesday evening prayer service. At this time all teachers and officers are required to be present if they are to be kept in their positions.

★ A WEEKLY VISITATION PROGRAM

Have a constant program of visiting the homes of all Sunday school members. Visit absentees at once. This can be done by the teacher at a time best suited to him or her, or through the regular weekly visitation program of the church. Through the visitation program, visit Sunday school prospects. Invite people to be present for a study of the Word of God.

Visitation is a great key to growth!

★ A CONSISTENT TEACHING PROGRAM

I am referring now to the teaching of the Bible in Sunday school on Sunday morning. In the presentation of the lesson, the teacher is at his best. The Word of God is the background for all of our teaching, and the goal of the teacher is to gain the interest of every pupil and to present him or her with the Word of God. Poor teaching is the reason why many Sunday schools fail. Teachers are to be prepared and dedicated to their jobs.

★ SET GOALS!

Be ever reaching greater numbers of people! Whatever the number may be in Sunday school on one Sunday, teacher, endeavor to reach more for the next Sunday. If the Sunday school is good for ten, it is good for ten thousand. For the Sunday school to grow, be constantly reaching for a goal—a definite goal.

23

Building
a Sunday School

Four Suggestions Shared With More Than 1500 Churches:

I. REACH ADULTS

To build a great Sunday school, reach adults! This means building strong adult classes.

Name the classes. Don't call them the "adult Bible class" or the "older adults" or "younger adults." Give them names such as Temple Bible Class, Victory Bible Class, Friendship Bible Class, Maranatha Bible Class. Or name the class after some great Christian of the past. Advertise the name. Tell people about it. Urge them to come and join.

Organize your class. Have a president, vice-president, secretary, treasurer and group captains. Use everyone you can to work in the class.

Advertise your class. Have calling cards made to hand out. Even put announcements in the papers. Use your telephone. Advertise everywhere.

II. TAKE A THOROUGH CENSUS OR SURVEY OF YOUR AREA

Cover a wide area. If you are in a small town, cover all of it. If you are in a big city, cover many blocks beyond your church. (In Chattanooga we covered Highland Park with a survey. One time we covered the entire city.)

Get hundreds of names of prospects. Prospects may be unsaved people or unaffiliated Baptists.

Write to these prospects every month. Make your letter friendly and offer them your services. A letter like that is better than a radio or TV announcement.

Visit your prospects quarterly. Be sure that a visit is made to every home on your list at least once per quarter.

Do your work with diligence, depending upon the Lord's guidance and the Holy Spirit's power.

III. INCREASE YOUR ENROLLMENT

Remember, anyone can join a Sunday school class. Sunday school is important. Why? You are teaching the Word of God.

Enroll the entire church in Sunday school. Don't ask them; simply enroll them. Every member of the church should be in Sunday school.

When people join your church by profession of faith or by letter, enroll them at once in Sunday school.

Keep the names on the roll. Don't remove them unless they die, move out of the city or join another church.

Follow up every absentee. Don't miss a one.

Always be concerned for the lost. If you have Sunday school members unsaved, pray for them and witness to them at every opportunity.

IV. USE BUSES

I recall so well when we had our first bus at Highland Park. We continued adding them until many buses were running every Sunday morning and bringing hundreds to Sunday school.

Keep your buses in good condition. Put the name of the church on the side of the bus.

Set goals for your buses.

Don't segregate your people. White or black, rich or poor, young or old—they are all people! Don't put bus people in a separate building and treat them as inferiors. Put them in the Sunday school classes with everyone else. And bring them to the church service. Be Christlike. Don't segregate. Remember the love of Christ for every sinner. He died for us all. And His concern still is for every sinner.

24

A Great Christian Leader . . .

. . . is positive about his salvation. Listen to the words of Paul:

"For the which cause I also suffer these things: nevertheless I am not ashamed: for I know whom I have believed, and am persuaded that he is able to keep that which I have committed unto him against that day."—II Tim. 1:12.

. . . is filled with the Spirit—yes, dead to self and filled with the Holy Spirit. Acts 4:31, "And they were all filled with the Holy Ghost, and they spake the word of God with boldness." And Acts 13:52, "The disciples were filled with joy, and with the Holy Ghost."

. . . knows the Bible. Yes, a great Christian leader knows the Word of God and preaches and teaches it. And his life is guided by it.

. . . has strong convictions. The men of God whose names are remembered so vividly had convictions—Joseph, Elijah, Daniel, Paul, and John—convictions about right and wrong.

. . . is concerned about others. Unselfishness is the keynote in a great Christian's life. He loves Christ, and he loves others.

Others, Lord, yes, others,
Let this my motto be;
Help me to live for others,
That I may live like Thee.

. . . *is steadfast in life.* "Therefore, my beloved brethren, be ye stedfast, unmoveable, always abounding in the work of the Lord, forasmuch as ye know that your labour is not in vain in the Lord" (I Cor. 15:58).

A great Christian is dependable, trustworthy, faithful.

. . . *is submissive to the will of God.* Our Saviour prayed, 'Father, Thy will be done'; we must pray the same prayer. In James 4:15 we read, "For that ye ought to say, If the Lord will, we shall live, and do this, or that."

If you are serious, sincere and seeking, God will make known His will for your life.

25

Be Your Best in Leadership

This simple outline is for preachers, singers, Sunday school workers, youth leaders, and all others interested and concerned about being your best in leadership.

I. BEING YOUR BEST IN LEADERSHIP

The three major problems are:

1. *Keeping yourself right.* This is a great imperative for a leader. If you are wrong in heart and spirit, everything else will go wrong. If you are wrong, you won't have the leadership or the power of God. So it is necessary that you be right with God and daily walk with Him. Your goal should always be to be filled with the Spirit.

2. *Stirring others.* Normally people do not want to be stirred. They prefer to live their lives in very relaxed and careless manner, unconcerned about others, content to let every man take his own course. This cannot be so for the Christian. Every child of God is to reach out and help someone else. Every leader is to stir others, to awaken them, to challenge them, to move them to action. This is not easy. Many people like the casual way of doing nothing. In our preaching or teaching, our goal should be to stir up those with whom we have contact.

3. *Staying on the main track.* For a Christian worker, the main track is concern for the salvation of others. This must ever be our longing, our passion, our desire. Do you want friends and loved ones to know Christ and be prepared to meet Him? Do you long for the whole world to hear the message of Christ and to come to Him for salvation?

The Devil would like to sidetrack all of us into doing secondary things, things not so important as winning souls. He would like us to emphasize social affairs and to minimize the need to reach others with the Gospel.

Staying on the main track is not only to win but to train people. A new Christian is a "babe in Christ" who needs training so he can grow in grace and effectively do work for his Saviour.

The three major problems, then, are keeping yourself right, stirring others, and staying on the main track.

II. BEING YOUR BEST IN HELPING OTHERS

Now to be your best in helping others, there are certain essentials:

1. *"Have faith in God"* (Mark 11:22)—the words of our Saviour. In this day of hustle and bustle, a day of clamoring for achievements, have faith in God.

Build your faith by constantly studying the Bible. Read the record of men of faith given us in Hebrews, chapter 11.

2. *Die to self.* Paul said, "I die daily." Your biggest enemy is self. Paul said, "Likewise reckon ye also yourselves to be dead indeed unto sin, but alive unto God through Jesus Christ our Lord" (Rom. 6:11).

Die to praise and to criticism. Nothing should turn you from the straight course of following Christ. Keep in mind that dying to self is a daily task. Your salvation is a single experience gained by faith in the Lord Jesus Christ, but dying to self is daily.

3. *Separate yourself from the love of money, selfish advancements and material gain.* The Lord Jesus put it in these words: "But seek ye first the kingdom of God, and his righteousness; and all these things shall be added unto you" (Matt. 6:33).

4. *Spend time in the Bible and in prayer.* Have a daily time when

you read the Word and pray. Pray with your family and loved ones. Pray before every meal. Pray before starting into a new project. Pray for faith, stamina and courage. I cannot emphasize too much the Word and prayer.

5. *Seek the salvation of the lost!* Pray for sinners to be saved. Tell them about Christ! Urge them to trust Him.

Every church should have a definite visitation program. This is a time when all members join together and go out to witness to the unsaved.

The central need of every person is salvation! The greatest experience that can come to anyone is to be born again and brought into the family of God by simple faith.

"For by grace are ye saved through faith; and that not of your-selves: it is the gift of God: Not of works, lest any man should boast." — Eph. 2:8, 9.

26

Attention, Bus Leaders!

1. *Take pride in your work.* Don't say, "I'm just a bus worker." You are a true leader, a bus evangelist working to bring men, women and children under the sound of the Gospel. Yours is a vitally important ministry in the winning of souls to Christ.

2. *Take advantage of soul-winning opportunities.* You will have them, even more than others. Now, don't overlook them. Speak tenderly and urgently to both young and old. Present the Gospel clearly. Do everything definitely and with a purpose.

Some people will ride your bus and hear the Gospel for the first time. Be sure they hear it plainly and in a definite way. Again, since some may be hearing the Gospel for the last time, do your best! Life is uncertain. Death is sure. Don't miss the opportunity of witnessing to others.

3. *Study people.* Study the young and the old. Diagnose their personalities, their problems. Put yourself in their place. Seek to know them. But at the same time, love them—even the worst of them. Keep in mind that one lost soul can become a precious, loving child of God.

4. *Brag on your church, your pastor, the staff.* Never criticize! Never laugh at your leaders. Give your full cooperation and help in every way to reach people and bring them under the sound of the Gospel.

There may be times when you want to criticize for some reason, but don't do it for the sake of those who need to know Christ.

5. *Refuse to be discouraged.* If you fail, get up and try again! We all fail at some time. Never are we perfect! Satan is always trying to turn us away from the major work. The world, the flesh and the Devil unite to throw stumbling blocks in our way and to make us want to give up. Keep pressing on!

6. *Be enthusiastic!* Put your best into your work! Get excited about your task. Someone said, "Nothing worthwhile is done without enthusiasm." I believe that to be true. For more than thirty years M. J. Parker headed the bus ministry of the Highland Park Baptist Church. And he was always enthusiastic.

7. *Set a good example.* Dress properly and be a good example of a dedicated Christian.

Set a good example in punctuality. Be on time in all your bus work. Keep in mind the hours of the services of the church. Help your people to be in place at the proper time.

Be concerned, compassionate and considerate of those who may have special problems.

8. *Win souls!* I keep repeating this. Jesus said, "And ye shall be witnesses unto me." Telling others of what Christ can do for them must always be our primary goal.

I was lost without Christ and a bus worker brought me to Sunday school. He did not have a bus as we have in this day, but he had an old Model-T Ford. He picked me up and took me to Sunday school. I sat in the class taught by Mrs. Daisy Hawes. I heard the Gospel for the first time. I left the class disturbed by what the teacher said.

The bus worker took me to Sunday school the second time in the Model-T Ford. I heard the Gospel again. After hearing it the second time, I received Christ as my Saviour.

Let us review a little bit. Look with me again: Be proud in your work; take advantage of soul-winning opportunities; study people; brag on your church, your pastor, your staff; refuse to be discouraged; be enthusiastic; set a good example; and, above all, win souls!

27

How to Build a Great Bible Class

A Bible class may be for men, for women, or for men and women. Concentrate on your task. Be prepared to face disappointments. Search for leaders to head up various aspects of the work.

First need: the pastor sold on the idea. You might be the teacher of the class, but get his approval and endorsement. If there is a need for an adult class of any kind in your church, then have a conference with your pastor.

Second need: a group to work with the teacher. The class may begin small, with two or three people. You can grow. Make plans to have a great, enthusiastic Bible class.

Third need: make plans for the class. Name the class—find an attractive, meaningful name, like the Temple Class, Grace Class, Friendship Class—you can think of hundreds more.

You need a few charter members to begin the Bible class—two, three, or half a dozen.

Get names of prospective members. By taking a census or surveying your community or the entire area around your church, find men and women who are not going to any church and invite them to your class. Make them welcome.

Start contacting people. Use the telephone. Write letters. Visit. Keep in touch with everyone.

Have a careful social program. This is not of primary importance, but it will do no harm. Let the class meet at times for a social, friendly gathering.

Fourth need: officers. I suggest the following: president, vice-president, secretary, treasurer, group captains. A group captain can have five, ten, or fifteen in his group. He will visit them, encourage them, and teach them to be faithful in attendance.

The class can also have some committees. These can be appointed by the officers to function in various ways. There may be committees for transportation, visitation, music and other class needs.

Fifth need: a weekly contact with all members. If a member of your class is absent on Sunday, have him contacted the following week. Dr. Beauchamp Vick taught a big class of many hundreds. Each week the group captains were to visit all absentees. They were instructed on how to minister to the needs of people and how to win souls to the Saviour.

Make your class one of compassion and personal concern for others.

Sixth need: to tie the class to all activities of the church. Do nothing in a Sunday school class that is contrary to the policy and program of the local church. Emphasize attendance at the regular services—Sunday morning, Sunday evening and Wednesday evening. The visitation program should be supported by every member.

These are just a few thoughts that might help in the building of an adult Sunday school class.

28

Characteristics of a Good Sunday School Worker

A Sunday school worker must be...

I. SAVED

1. *A Sunday school worker must be saved in order to understand the Bible.* "But the natural man receiveth not the things of the Spirit of God: for they are foolishness unto him: neither can he know them, because they are spiritually discerned," declares I Corinthians 2:14. No teacher or worker can know and understand the Bible without the aid of the Holy Spirit. The Spirit is our guide into all truth (John 16:13).

2. *A Sunday school worker must be saved in order to have the right influence.* No man is good who shuts Christ out of his life, either by rejection or by negligence and indifference. It is Christ who gives a radiant, telling influence. Without Him the influence is warped and misleading.

Every Sunday school worker must reckon with this matter of influence. Others are following you, looking at you. "For none of us liveth to himself, and no man dieth to himself" (Rom. 14:7).

Let Christ shine through your life to bless others and to glorify God. "Let your light so shine before men, that they may see your good works, and glorify your Father which is in heaven" (Matt. 5:16).

3. *A Sunday school worker must be saved to harmonize with the purpose of the Sunday school.* The Sunday school is for the teaching of the Word of God. It is not an organization for social enjoyment. It is for teaching the Bible and enlightening darkened souls.

An unsaved teacher may think the purpose of the Sunday school is simply to entertain boys and girls, men and women, for thirty or forty minutes and then send them on their way. No! The Sunday school is for the teaching of the Bible. And this can be accomplished only by saved and consecrated teachers.

4. *A Sunday school teacher must be saved in order to win others.* A knowledge of your own salvation is necessary if you are to help another get saved. D. L. Moody often said, "No man can win souls unless he himself is saved and knows it." So you must be able to say, "Christ is my Saviour, the Lord is my Shepherd, my Lord, my God."

C. T. Studd, an eminent missionary of years gone by, said to a lady in England, "Salvation is like smallpox: when you have it, you give it to others." The lady was at first offended but then was led of the Spirit to recognize her spiritual condition and need.

Some time later Studd received a telegram from her that read:

> HAVE A BAD CASE OF SMALLPOX. PRAISE GOD!
> DOLLY

Spurgeon said, "God will not use dead tools for working living miracles."

An experience of redeeming grace is necessary if you are to lead others to Christ.

A good Sunday school worker is...

II. SEPARATED

Too few people know the Bible definition of separation. Some think it refers to our attitude toward the world. If we refrain from engaging in certain worldly practices, we are living the "separated life." This is only half of the meaning.

Separation means separation from the world and to the Lord and His work. Separation implies a dedication to the full purpose of God. Perhaps the best verses to picture the positive and negative of this matter are Romans 12:1, 2.

"I beseech you therefore, brethren, by the mercies of God, that ye present your bodies a living sacrifice, holy, acceptable unto God, which is your reasonable service. And be not conformed to this world: but be ye transformed by the renewing of your mind, that ye may prove what is that good, and acceptable, and perfect, will of God."

Paul here represents the positive call first. This is right; for when we give ourselves wholly to God, it isn't difficult to say "no" to the world.

Consider the following:

1. *Separation is a Bible doctrine.* It is taught from the first of Genesis to the last of Revelation. It is illustrated in the obedient life of Abraham. It is pictured in the separation of Israel from other nations.

2. *Separation is absolutely necessary if one is to be filled with the Spirit.* The Holy Spirit will not fill and empower one entangled with the affairs of this world. Nor will the Holy Spirit fill an unsurrendered individual. The Lord will not use an unclean, unsurrendered vessel. Therefore, if one is not separated from the world, he disobeys the command, "Be filled with the Spirit"; he lives beneath the standard God has for him; and he fails to be an instrument for good in the hands of God.

3. *Separation calls for the best.* It requires a definite stand. It brings forth the opposition of the world, but it also brings the peace of God.

4. *Separation fits one for the greatest work—soul winning.* Without separation, positive and negative, there is little concern for souls. Without separation, there is no power for this task. Without separation, the lost world will be able to point a finger at you and say, "Hypocrite!"

The call of God is "Wherefore come out from among them, and be ye separate, saith the Lord, and touch not the unclean thing." Study carefully II Corinthians 6:11–18.

A good Sunday school worker . . .

III. PRAYS

The command is "Pray without ceasing." A good Sunday school worker will obey this command. He will realize that only through prayer can he accomplish the work given to him.

As Sunday school workers, for what should we pray?

1. *For an understanding of the Bible.* Never approach a study of the Bible without a prayer in your heart. The deeper meanings of the Word are revealed to those who approach the Book prayerfully. In studying the Sunday school lesson, pray for understanding.

2. *For the salvation of the lost.* The Sunday schoolteacher who is not interested in the winning of lost souls will be a dry, matter-of-fact teacher who will soon lose the interest of the saved. If every member of your class is a Christian, then have the class go out after those who are unsaved. In every class, offer prayer for those who are out of the ark of safety.

3. *For the building up of professing Christians.* The admonition of the Scripture is "Grow in grace, and in the knowledge of our Lord and Saviour Jesus Christ." It is not enough to lead people to an acceptance of Jesus Christ. We must help them grow. The worker must pray for the stabilizing of the members of the class or department.

4. *For the solution of class and department problems.* No Sunday school organization will ever be free from problems and difficulties. As long as we are working with people, we will have problems. The solution to every problem can be found in fervent prayer.

Are you perplexed and troubled now about some problem in your class or department? Take your burden to the Lord and leave it there.

5. *For the strengthening of our own lives.* Teaching a class of young children is too great for any of us. We have to have the help of God. We are doomed to failure if we try to work in our own strength. Paul said, "I can do all things through Christ which strengtheneth me."

"Pray without ceasing." The best trained teacher is a failure if he does not pray. The finest, best organized class is dead without prayer. The most efficient class officer or department leader is a miserable failure without prayer.

A good Sunday school worker...

IV. PLANS

To plan is to organize your efforts for future work. This is what the architect does, the artist, the farmer—and the successful Christian worker.

Joseph worked by a God-given plan in the days of Egypt's plenty and famine. Nehemiah worked by a definite plan in the rebuilding of the walls of Jerusalem. Nehemiah has been called "a model organizer." In the rebuilding of the city, he used three grand principles: division of labor; cooperation; concentration.

The Apostle Paul made plans in his spiritual work by writing ahead to the churches and revealing his plans.

Our Heavenly Father has a definite plan for the future. This plan includes the second coming, the millennial kingdom, and finally, the new Heaven and the new earth.

For successful work plan ahead. But make your plans in the light of God's plan. Always say, "If the Lord will, we shall live, and do this, or that" (James 4:15). Also, make your plans in the light of the return of Christ. Since He may come at any moment, we should eagerly be looking.

Pray about your plans. Seek the leadership of the Holy Spirit. Be sure that all are harmonious with the Bible. May we not be guilty of planning ahead, as did the rich fool of Luke 12, and leave God out.

1. *Make plans to the glory of God.* Whatever you do, seek to please the Heavenly Father and to honor His holy name. Selfish plans will not glorify Him; neither will small, stingy, fearful plans.

2. *Make plans so that you can better utilize your life.* Without plans, time is wasted, opportunities are lost, and talents are neglected. Life is short; avail yourself of every moment. Careful planning will enable you to accomplish far more.

3. *Make plans for the blessing of others.* Christian workers should keep before them the main goals—the reaching of the lost and the strengthening of the saved. With this twofold goal, make careful plans.

Finally, if God be in your plans, make them big! "All things are possible to him that believeth."

Hold to your plans. Hold to them until you see their fulfillment. When your plans have accomplished their purpose, then let them go—AND MAKE OTHERS!

A good Sunday school worker is...

V. FAITHFUL

What is being faithful? It is doing your best in whatever God has given you to do. It matters not whether the task be great or small, being faithful is a prerequisite for best work. Good Sunday school workers are faithful whether they be teachers, officers, secretaries, song leaders, group captains or do other work.

Doing your best means being faithful in attendance, rain or shine, summer or winter. Faithfulness is essential.

Doing your best means being faithful in preparation. There is so much slouchy preparation for Christian work. The world believes in preparation, whether it be in politics, business, the professions or the arts. Years are spent in preparing for a given work. Too often unprepared people are given positions of great responsibility in the church and Sunday school. This is not as sad as the fact that the unprepared make no effort to improve their knowledge or technique of work.

Surely ours is the greatest work in the world. The need is for faithful, skilled, prepared laborers.

Remember the following:

1. *God demands faithfulness:* "Moreover it is required in stewards, that a man be found faithful" (I Cor. 4:2).

2. *God blesses faithfulness.* Observe how He blessed Abraham, Joshua, Paul and Job. The Word indicates that blessings are given here and hereafter to the faithful. Note the great loss suffered by the unfaithful (Matt. 25:14–30).

3. *God delights in faithfulness.* It should be the desire of every Christian to please God. Nothing pleases Him more than faithfulness in life and in work. Study carefully the life of Abraham, and you will see why he was called "the father of the faithful."

4. *Faithfulness produces results.* Whether a man's talents be one or five, in the end he will do a most worthy work if he is faithful. Will the Lord say to you, "Well done, good and faithful servant"?

A good Sunday school worker...

VI. STUDIES

Seneca said, "If you devote your time to study, you will avoid all irksomeness of life; nor will you long for the approach of night, being tired of the day; nor will you be a burden to yourself, nor your society insupportable to others."

May we adapt this thought to the Sunday school worker. If he devotes himself to a study of the Word, the following will be true:

1. *He will be alert.* The mind will be active. The heart will be stirred. Intellectual and spiritual drowsiness will disappear.

2. *He will grow in grace and knowledge.* The Apostle Peter exhorts us, "But grow in grace, and in the knowledge of our Lord and Saviour Jesus Christ" (II Pet. 3:18).

3. *He will be a blessing to others.* When the Bible is taken into your life, there will be an overflow into the lives of others. Devoted Bible teachers shed abroad an influence which tells for eternity.

The main purpose of the Sunday school is to study the Bible. This purpose is realized only when the leaders of classes and departments give themselves to the study of it.

Bible Study Demands the Following:

1. *A love for the Bible.* No one should engage in Sunday school work who cannot honestly say that he loves the Word of God. The curse is on the one who likes the spotlight prominence of teaching but has no love for the Bible. If a genuine love for the Word is lacking in your life, give yourself to prayer until this be corrected.

2. *Prayer.* To know our Bibles, we must pray for the Holy Spirit to illumine our minds. This Book is inspired by the Holy Spirit; it is the Sword of the Spirit; therefore, the Holy Spirit can help us to an understanding of the Word. Prayer and study go together.

3. *Concentration.* Literally force yourself to concentrate on the study of the Word. The Devil will seek to turn you away. The treasures of the Word are revealed to those who give themselves to concentrated study.

Suggestions for Preparing Sunday School Lessons:

1. *Start in time.* Too many teachers put off the study of the lesson until the last minute.

2. *Read the lesson many times.* Study what comes before and after the selected Scripture lesson.

3. *Outline the lesson so the truth can be grasped and retained.*

A good Sunday school worker...

VII. VISITS

This is a new and difficult day in Sunday school work. Many things clamor for the interest of young and old. The radio, television, good highways, fast cars, high tension living—all seek to lead people away from God, the church and Sunday school. But there is victory through prayer, consistent living and hard work.

Visitation is work! Yes, there is a pleasure in visiting, but it will often be hard work. To win people to Christ and establish them in the Faith is the prime objective of the Sunday school. Satan's desire is to defeat this purpose; therefore, he will oppose visitation.

The Lord Jesus practiced and taught visitation. Observe Christ in the homes of the sick, the sorrowing, the sinful. He taught visitation when He sent out His disciples and gave them directions regarding their visitation work. The Apostle Paul believed in and practiced visitation. He said regarding his ministry in Ephesus, ". . . and have taught you publickly, and from house to house."

What Visitation Does:

1. *Warms the teacher's (worker's) heart.* The heart of a teacher becomes cold when there is no contact with the pupil. Visitation

makes better Sunday school teachers. It provides illustrations and reveals the needs of others.

2. *Shows the interest of the teacher in the pupil.* All people like to know that somebody cares. When the teacher or worker takes time to visit, the pupil is strengthened and helped. Indifference is the enemy which robs Sunday schools and dwarfs the souls of many. Good, sane visitation stirs the indifferent and brings them back to the house of God.

3. *Solves problems.* Quite often problems arise in a Sunday school department or class. Feelings are hurt, entire families are affected. Sensible, kindly visitation will help solve problems and bring people together in the spirit of the Lord. The visitor should pray much, both before and during a visit. Prayer changes people and things.

4. *Brings souls to Christ.* Public preaching is important, but visitation for the sake of winning souls is equally important. At least eighty percent of all who respond to the public invitation have been dealt with in personal interviews by workers. What years of preaching cannot do, a few minutes of visitation will accomplish. So Sunday school worker, study carefully the art of soul winning.

5. *Increases the enrollment and attendance, both in Sunday school and church.* Any class or department can grow when visitation is consistently done. The world's greatest Sunday schools have been built through visitation.

6. *Makes use of the only tried and true method for building a Sunday school and winning souls.* Newspaper advertising is good; radio announcements accomplish much; but visitation has proved to be the one successful way to grow a Sunday school.

7. *Brings the greatest dividends.* One hour of visitation may result in the salvation of lost souls, strengthening of weak Christians, the uniting of a home, and the changing of a score of lives.

A good Sunday school worker is...

VIII. ENTHUSIASTIC

There is no success without enthusiasm! Webster tells us that enthusiasm is ardent zeal or interest—fervor.

David Livingstone, the pioneer missionary, said, "Nothing good or great has ever been accomplished in this world without enthusiasm."

Clarence Macartney comments, "Without enthusiasm, no battles have been won, no cathedrals built, no empires founded, no religions propagated. The secret of success is enthusiasm. The men of victory have been the men who kept the fires burning on the altars of enthusiasm when other flames had sunk into cold gray ashes of despair."

The world knows the value of enthusiasm. Success comes to men in business, professions and politics when they are enthusiastic and wholehearted. Campaigns of Hitler and Mussolini were characterized by great enthusiasm. Communists were enthusiastic in the spread of their hellish teachings.

But what about Christians? So many are lukewarm, indifferent, half dead. We have the greatest message in the world! Too often we present it in such a half-hearted way that people do not listen. False religionists are always enthusiastic, but the followers of Christ too often lack this necessary characteristic.

What does enthusiasm do?

Enthusiasm generates confidence. When you are enthusiastically sold out to your work, it brings the confidence of others.

It brushes aside opposition. When a surging fervor possesses the soul, opposition will receive little recognition.

It is contagious. An enthusiastic Sunday school worker can stir and inspire all of the people around him.

Enthusiasm builds Sunday school classes, Sunday school departments—entire Sunday schools! Pray for a holy enthusiasm. The Apostle Paul had it, and he exhorts us in Romans 12:11 to be "Not slothful in business; fervent in spirit; serving the Lord."

A good Sunday school worker...

IX. ATTENDS THE WEEKLY TEACHERS' AND OFFICERS' MEETING

In a big business, the heads of the departments meet together for consultation. In the army, the officers meet often for staff meetings. In a school, the faculty is brought together frequently for discussion of the work.

In the successful operation of a great Sunday school, the weekly meeting of the teachers and officers is indispensable. Because of the importance of this meeting, no teacher nor elected officer is allowed to hold office without faithful attendance.

The weekly teachers' and officers' meeting supplies the following:

1. *Methods for successful Sunday school building.* We can always improve our way of doing things. We need to know the best methods for arousing interest and increasing attendance in our individual classes.

2. *An opportunity for teamwork.* Paul says we are "workers together with him." We are co-laborers. To build a successful Sunday school, we must pull in the same direction. It is by cooperation and teamwork that buildings are erected, wars are won, and the wheels of progress are kept turning.

3. *Inspiration for the task.* The work of the teacher is often discouraging. The unfaithfulness of pupils, the indifference of parents, the carelessness of youth, all blend together to present a difficult task. Satan opposes the work of a consecrated Sunday school teacher. A time is needed each week to give and receive inspiration.

4. *Instruction in the Word.* Every teachers' meeting supplies some guidance in the problem of presenting the Word of God. Difficulties are ironed out, the point of emphasis for the next Sunday's lesson is specified.

Is the weekly meeting of teachers and officers important? To assist you in answering this, may I suggest two other questions. Can you name two successful Sunday schools that don't have such a meeting? Can you name a successful Sunday school class directed by teachers and officers who ignore the importance of this weekly meeting?

THE SEVEN LAWS OF TEACHING

The Seven Laws of Teaching by John Gregory was first published in 1884. His principles are still regarded highly today.

A. *The Law of the Teacher—Know*

The teacher needs to know:

1. The Lord personally.
2. The pupil intimately.
3. The Bible comprehensively.
4. The lesson thoroughly.

B. *The Law of the Learner—Attention*

The learner must attend with interest the material to be learned.

1. First, you must gain and hold attention.
2. Problems to the holding of attention:
   a. Too much teacher talk, loud, monotonous voice, serious tones.
   b. Lack of promptness; lack of preparation of lesson; lack of materials.
   c. Listening or talking to one pupil for any length of time.

C. *The Law of Language—Common to Both*

Language is the medium of communication between the pupil and teacher. Thus:

1. It must be understood by both.
2. It must have the same meaning for both (symbolism is not understood by the young child).

D. *The Law of the Lesson—Known to Unknown*

The truth to be taught must be learned through truth already known.

1. Start where the pupil is, but go somewhere; learning must advance.
2. Proceed by graded steps.
3. Illuminate by illustration.

E. *The Law of the Teaching Process—Use Pupil's Mind*

The teacher must awaken and set in action the mind of the pupil, arousing his self-activities.

True teaching is not that which gives knowledge, but that which stimulates pupils to gain it.

F. *The Law of the Learning Process—**Think, Feel, Put Into Action***

The pupil must reproduce in his own mind the truth to be learned.

True learning is not memorization and repetition of the words and ideas of the teacher.

G. *The Law of Review and Application—**Draw the Net; Be Doers of the Word***

29

Paul's Convictions About the Work of the Christian

"For what is our hope, or joy, or crown of rejoicing? Are not even ye in the presence of our Lord Jesus Christ at his coming?" —I Thess. 2:19.

Paul's main objective was to present Christ the Saviour. His love for Christ pressed this objective upon him. He knew the saving power of the Son of God.

His knowledge of the Word laid upon him the presentation of Christ as the only Saviour. He knew the teaching of Heaven and Hell. He knew the way of salvation through the Son of God.

Paul had rugged convictions. He did not hesitate to express his convictions.

He was opposed to troublemakers. They upset him. In I Timothy 1:20 he mentioned two troublemakers by name: Hymenaeus and Alexander.

He was strong in the denunciation of the worldly. In II Timothy 4:10, he said: "For Demas hath forsaken me, having loved this present world, and is departed unto Thessalonica. . . . "

Paul was upset by quitters. It took him a long time to "get over" the action of John Mark, the youth who went with Paul and Barnabas on their first missionary journey. But when they came to Perga, in Pamphylia, he turned back. Paul later had a serious argument with Barnabas about Mark's quitting instincts.

Paul had convictions about Christian service, convictions which came from the Lord. He believed that every Christian should be a witness for the Saviour. The commission of the Son of God was upon him.

"And Jesus came and spake unto them, saying, All power is given unto me in heaven and in earth.

"Go ye therefore, and teach all nations, baptizing them in the name of the Father, and of the Son, and of the Holy Ghost:

"Teaching them to observe all things whatsoever I have command-ed you: and, lo, I am with you alway, even unto the end of the world. Amen."—Matt. 28:18-20.

Because of this commission, Paul felt his first task was the proclamation of the Gospel—"The Good News of Jesus Christ"—and the winning of souls.

As I thought of this theme and of Paul's convictions regarding the major work of the Christian, this outline presented itself to me.

I. OUR TASK

We are to bring others to Christ as Andrew brought Simon Peter. Andrew himself first found Christ, then led his brother to Christ. I don't know that Andrew ever preached a sermon; if he did, it is not recorded. But he did a great day's work when he led Peter to Jesus. Peter preached on the Day of Pentecost, and three thousand came to Christ.

But what if Andrew had failed in his personal work? Thank God he didn't!

Mr. Edward Kimball of Boston led D. L. Moody to the Lord. But had Mr. Kimball failed, we do not know that we would have the record of the great Moody revivals and the many sermons by him.

Thank God for personal work! I believe in great preaching, but often we can do more by personal work than by pulpit preaching.

1. *Soul winning is primary for the preacher of the Gospel.* It is

his responsibility to give the message of Christ in such a way that others will be brought to the Saviour. The pastor must show he cares in the execution of his ministry. We have been called to be fishers of men. A care for souls will help us frame our sermons. A passion for souls will show itself in the choice of messages. A passion for the lost will stir our energy and direct us in all our contacts with men.

2. *Soul winning is primary for the Sunday schoolteacher.* In the commission, our Saviour commanded two kinds of teaching: the teaching that wins men to Christ—evangelistic, soul-winning instruction—and soul-building, character-constructing teaching. One wins the faith, the affections and the spiritual loyalty to Christ as Redeemer; the other wins the whole man to Christ's doctrines, program and world plans.

It is the business of the superintendent and all the teachers to be watching for souls. It is important that we see that men and women and children are lost without Christ; and it is our business to point them to Him.

3. *Soul winning is the business of the training union.* We are training young people to serve, and the greatest service is the winning of souls.

4. *Soul winning is the business of the deacons.* The Bible says, "For they that have used the office of a deacon well purchase to themselves a good degree, and great boldness in the faith which is in Christ Jesus" (I Tim. 3:13).

Every deacon ought to be a soul winner—and every deacon can be a soul winner if he tries. Out of the seven deacons of the first church at Jerusalem, two became unordained evangelists. The dying testimony of Stephen started conviction in the heart of Saul of Tarsus and doubtless led to his conversion. Philip held a great meeting in Samaria and led to Christ the treasurer of an African kingdom.

We expect much of each deacon. He must live different from the people around him. His life must show forth the Lord Jesus Christ. He must be good, pure, clean, consecrated. Deacons must be so spiritual that they are constantly concerned about others. It is my prayer that all eighty of the deacons at Highland Park will win souls. It is our plan for the future to organize our deacons into definite groups to go out and bring others to the Saviour.

5. *Soul winning is the primary business of the ushers, for the choir members, for the orchestra; yes, soul winning is for everybody—the young and the old.*

Our task: the winning of men, women and children to Christ.

II. OUR BOOK

"All scripture is given by inspiration of God, and is profitable for doctrine, for reproof, for correction, for instruction in righteousness." —II Tim. 3:16.

The Holy Bible is given to us to be used for the winning of men to Christ. The Bible has all we need. By the Word of God we can witness to others. By the Word of God we can win people to Jesus Christ.

A fine lad came and told me of his joy in the Saviour. He said that, above all, he wanted to be a soul winner. He wanted me to give him the names of books that would give the teachings of various denominations and certain of the cults and isms of this day.

I asked the young man if he had read the Bible through. No, he had not, because he had been saved only a short time. I told him that I thought he should read the Bible from cover to cover and carefully absorb as much as he could for his benefit and for the benefit of others. I then stated that, after he had read the Bible through, I would give him the names of books that he could read to inform him about the various religions of the world.

The young man has not been back to see me—doubtless he has not read the Bible through as yet. It may be that he will discover so much in the Bible that he will soon see he doesn't need all of the teachings of the various religions of the world.

The Bible is the Book that we must use in winning souls!

The Word produces convictions. The inspired Bible will bring men to where they will see their lost condition.

The Word regenerates. When the Bible is given and the Holy Spirit works, then regeneration takes place.

The Word produces faith. "So then faith cometh by hearing, and hearing by the word of God."

Dr. R. A. Torrey said five texts ought to sink deep into the heart of every personal worker. They are:

"So then faith cometh by hearing, and hearing by the word of God."—Rom. 10:17.

"The seed is the word of God."—Luke 8:11.

"Being born again, not of corruptible seed, but of incorruptible, by the word of God, which liveth and abideth for ever."—I Pet. 1:23.

"And take the helmet of salvation, and the sword of the Spirit, which is the word of God."—Eph. 6:17.

"Is not my word like as a fire? saith the Lord; and like a hammer that breaketh the rock in pieces?"—Jer. 23:29.

If the soul winner does not depend on the Word of God, he is doomed to failure. We must know how to use the Word of God for definite results. A great many have a large theoretical knowledge of the Bible but no practical knowledge. They don't know how to take the Word of God and point a man to the Saviour.

The Bible is yours. Use it to help others to Christ.

III. OUR ADVERSARY

Keep in mind that we are talking about Paul's convictions regarding the work of the Christian. We have established already that our main business is to point people to the Lamb of God who takes away the sin of the world. We consider now the adversary:

"Lest Satan should get an advantage of us: for we are not ignorant of his devices."—II Cor. 2:11.

"Be sober, be vigilant; because your adversary the devil, as a roaring lion, walketh about, seeking whom he may devour."—I Pet. 5:8.

Satan is the enemy of soul winning! He will tolerate singing, formal worship, fellowship and Bible reading; but he hates our soul winning. Someone said: "The cry of theologians that God is dead proves very much that the Devil is alive!"

1. *Satan diverts churches.* Sometimes the church may be known as a good, fundamental, New Testament church; but that church may have turned away from the main business—winning souls.

I was in such a church where they had gone thirteen months without having a soul saved and without baptizing a convert. The pastor was fundamental. The church was known as a very fundamental, conservative church; yet they had turned away from the passion of soul winning. The Devil was in control. They believed the Book, they studied the Book, but they had departed from the main teaching of the Book.

The early church was evangelistic. Soul winning was its chief work.

2. *Satan diverts individuals from soul winning.* When people get saved, they should have a concern for others. But strangely, after a time, the Devil diverts people from the main business. Quite often when a man gets in a church and gets busy in a certain job, he turns away from winning the lost.

Sometimes the Devil will use certain people to divert the attention of others from soul winning. Here is what Paul had to say about this matter in Romans 16:17: "Now I beseech you, brethren, mark them which cause divisions and offences contrary to the doctrine which ye have learned; and avoid them."

Paul went on to say that some people are not serving the Lord but serving their own interests. He stated that "by good words and fair speeches [they] deceive the hearts of the simple."

Yes, Satan discourages the soul winner. And constant failure to win the lost often causes people to cease their soul-winning efforts.

When people get discouraged in soul winning, it is easy for the Devil to cause them to lead careless lives. They forget the admonition of the Scripture, "Come out from among them, and be ye separate, saith the Lord." They forget the words of the Lord Jesus, "Ye cannot serve God and mammon." But, oh, what a blessing when Christians live for God!

We had in our church Lambert Mims, once mayor of Mobile, Alabama. He was a great witness for Christ. At twenty-five years of age, he lost his company because of drinking and bad business involvements. He found a job as a representative in a flour company and continued his drinking. One of his closest drinking buddies was Joe Pope, an employee of one of the flour company's customers. One day when they met, Mims offered Pope a drink. But he refused, saying, "I don't intend to touch liquor again as long as I live." Joe Pope simply explained that he had been converted in a revival meeting.

In the weeks that followed, Mims called his friend "Holy Joe" and ridiculed him in every possible way. Pope kept smiling back. One day when he suggested that Mims should get saved and give God a chance in his life, Mims retorted in anger, "Don't talk to me anymore about religion. I don't need it."

Joe Pope kept on smiling and witnessing to Lambert Mims. Then one day Pope was killed in a tragic head-on auto accident. When Lambert Mims viewed his friend's broken body, his mind was in a daze. The crash had been so severe that Pope had been thrown through the windshield with a force, pulling him out of his shoes. But a smile remained on his face! Mims never forgot his friend's smile. He thought of the decision he knew he had to make.

Finally, one day when he was depressed, he stopped his car on the side of the road, fell on his knees and asked God to save him. Of course, salvation was his at once. Later, Lambert Mims was elected mayor of his city and became "Alabama's Outstanding Young Man."

The thing that woke him up was Joe Pope's constant testimony for Christ and the smile on his face.

Christian, live so that others can see Christ in you.

IV. OUR PROBLEM

The big problem is self! Paul recognized this and said, "Likewise reckon ye also yourselves to be dead indeed unto sin, but alive unto God through Jesus Christ our Lord" (Rom. 6:11). He said, "For ye are dead, and your life is hid with Christ in God" (Col. 3:3).

Four things come from following self:

1. *Following self leads to laziness.* Lazy Christians troubled the apostle (II Thess. 3).

2. *Following self leads to a disruption of Christian service.* When people follow self, they are never steady in their service. They don't attend the services of the church faithfully. Following self causes men to get offended easily. Following self will cause one to turn from his path of duty.

3. *Following the flesh leads to false teaching.* A pastor called me from a distant city. His people were torn up by a fly-by-night false teacher. He said that they were disturbed by the teacher's ideas about the opening chapters of Genesis. They had become so engrossed in the teachings of this man that they had turned away from their pastor and from their church.

4. *Following self leads to fleshly sins; thereby, soul winning is defeated.* God cannot use the worldly and unseparated person. In II Timothy 2:19–21 we find these words,

"Nevertheless the foundation of God standeth sure, having this seal, The Lord knoweth them that are his. And, Let every one that nameth the name of Christ depart from iniquity.

"But in a great house there are not only vessels of gold and of silver, but also of wood and of earth; and some to honour, and some to dishonour.

"If a man therefore purge himself from these, he shall be a vessel unto honour, sanctified, and meet for the master's use, and prepared unto every good work."

There will always be a battle with self, but we can win the battle! We can die to self and be made alive unto God, thereby bringing forth fruit!

I refer you again to a favorite verse of mine found in John 12:24: "Verily, verily, I say unto you, Except a corn of wheat fall into the ground and die, it abideth alone: but if it die, it bringeth forth much fruit."

V. OUR HELPER

One who dwells within us is our Helper in the soul-winning project. In Acts 1:8 we read: "But ye shall receive power, after that the Holy Ghost is come upon you...." We have One abiding in us who is ready to help us and desires to fill us with power and use us.

Do you know the meaning of the fullness of the Spirit? Have you seriously thought on this matter? Allow me to suggest to you again that the fullness of the Spirit is dependent upon two things: emptiness of self and willingness to be used of Him.

The one concern of the Devil is to keep Christians from praying. If you want God to use you in winning others, then let nothing hinder you from a fervent prayer life. We must ask God to bring us to the ones whom we can help. We must ask God to give us the words to say to them. Every word must be based upon the Scripture, but we need particular words for particular individuals.

We must pray that God will give us power to speak His message to others. If there is anything we need in this age of hurry and rush, it is prayer. James tells us: "Ye lust, and have not: ye kill, and desire to have, and cannot obtain: ye fight and war, yet ye have not, because ye ask not" (James 4:2). The soul winner must not neglect the place of prayer. If we are to get through to God, we must ask, seek and knock.

Isaiah tells us: "But they that wait upon the Lord shall renew their strength; they shall mount up with wings as eagles; they shall run, and not be weary; and they shall walk, and not faint" (40:31).

The Holy Spirit is our Helper in soul winning; and prayer is the instrument whereby we touch the throne of God.

VI. OUR REWARD

The soul winner has a twofold reward coming to him—now and hereafter.

The greatest joy that any Christian can have is the joy of winning others to Christ. Many have experienced this joy and know the full meaning of it.

But there is more. At the judgment seat we shall be rewarded also.

Many so-called Christian activities don't merit even a mentioning at the judgment seat, but soul winning will assuredly come before Him.

We must witnesss in love. We must witness willingly. We must

___ unselfishly. We must witness faithfully.

You have heard me speak many times of the man known as Uncle John Vassar.

One day a student was coming down the road and met a man who was somewhat crippled. The boy asked, "What's your business, Mister?"

The man grinned and replied, "I am looking for some lost sheep."

The boy hurried home to tell his parents about the crazy man looking for sheep. But his parents replied, "Why, that's Uncle John Vassar, the missionary, searching for people to win to Christ."

Uncle John had been a brewery worker before he was converted. Conscience forced him to quit his job. Then his wife and two children died. But still trusting in Christ, Uncle John resolved to spend the rest of his life winning lost sheep. He went from church to church. He won literally thousands.

Uncle John called himself "The Shepherd's Dog." He belonged to the Lord, and he was seeking out the sheep that he could bring to the Saviour. When he died in 1878, he was eulogized as the most skillful personal soul winner in America.

In discussing Paul's conviction about the work of the Christian, we have seen that our business is to win souls.

We have before us Paul's example as a soul winner. As he went from place to place, he was constantly telling the story of Jesus and pointing people to the Saviour.

We are exhorted by Paul's life and by the fervency of his message to bring others to Christ. For the people of Israel, Paul said, "I have great heaviness and continual sorrow in my heart."

We have Paul's examination, an examination coming for all of us at the judgment seat of Christ. In Romans 14:10 we are told that "we shall all stand before the judgment seat of Christ." There we will give account of ourselves to Him. The biggest accounting will be regarding the winning of others to Christ.

Oh, to be found faithful in this task!

For a complete list of books available from the Sword of the Lord, write to Sword of the Lord Publishers, P. O. Box 1099, Murfreesboro, Tennessee 37133.